Critical Acclaim for Laura Pedersen

Buffalo Gal

"This book is compulsively readable, and owes its deadpan delivery to the fact that she has performed standup comedy on national television (*The Oprah Winfrey Show, Late Night with David Letterman, Today, Primetime,* etc.)."

—*ForeWord Magazine*

Best Bet

"The book's laugh-out-loud funny, and readers will find themselves rereading lines just for the sheer joy of it."

—*Kirkus Reviews*

The Big Shuffle

"Although it's a laugh-out-loud read, it's an appealing, sensitive, superbly written book. One you won't want to put down. I loved it."

—*The Lakeland Times*

"Be prepared to fall in love with a story as wise as it is witty."

—*The Compulsive Reader*

The Sweetest Hours

"To call *The Sweetest Hours* a book of short stories would be like calling the *Mona Lisa* a painting."

—*Front Street Reviews*

"Pedersen weaves tales that blen   rise endings in the games of life and

.oons

Heart's Desire

"Funny, tender, and poignant, *Heart's Desire* should appeal to a wide range of readers."

—*Booklist*

"Prepare to fall in love again because Laura Pedersen is giving you your 'Heart's Desire' by bringing back Hallie Palmer and her entire endearing crew. In a story as wise as it is witty, Pedersen captures the joy of love found, the ache of love lost, and how friends can get you through it all—win or lose."

—Sarah Bird, author of *The Yokota Officers Club*

"This book will make you laugh and cry and like a good friend, you'll be happy to have made its acquaintance."

—Lorna Landvik, author of *Angry Housewives Eating Bon Bons*

Last Call

"Pedersen writes vividly of characters so interesting, so funny and warm that they defy staying on the page."

—*The Hartford Courant*

"This book is a rare, humorous exploration of death that affirms life is a gift and tomorrow is never guaranteed. Pedersen writes an exquisitely emotional story. A must-have book to start the new year."

—*Romantic Times*

Beginner's Luck

"Laura Pedersen delivers…if this book hasn't been made into a screenplay already, it should be soon. Throughout, you can't help but think how hilarious some of the scenes would play on the big screen."

—*The Hartford Courant*

"Funny, sweet-natured, and well-crafted…Pedersen has created a wonderful assemblage of…whimsical characters and charm."

—*Kirkus Reviews*

Also by Laura Pedersen

Nonfiction
Play Money
Buffalo Gal

Fiction
Going Away Party
Beginner's Luck
Last Call
Heart's Desire
The Sweetest Hours
The Big Shuffle
Best Bet

www.LauraPedersenBooks.com

Buffalo Unbound

Buffalo Unbound

A Celebration

Laura Pedersen

FULCRUM
GOLDEN, COLORADO

Library of Congress Cataloging-in-Publication Data

Pedersen, Laura.
 Buffalo unbound / Laura Pedersen.
  p. cm.
 ISBN 978-1-55591-735-7 (pbk.)
 1. Buffalo (N.Y.)--History. 2. Buffalo (N.Y.)--Social life and customs. 3. Buffalo (N.Y.)--Biography. I. Title.
 F129.B857P43 2010
 974.7'97043--dc22

                              2010014920

Printed on recycled paper in Canada by Friesens Corp.
0 9 8 7 6 5 4 3 2 1

Design by Jack Lenzo
Cover photo © Jim Bush, www.jimbushphotography.com

Fulcrum Publishing
4690 Table Mountain Drive, Suite 100
Golden, Colorado 80403
800-992-2908 • 303-277-1623
www.fulcrumbooks.com

I think when you die, your soul goes to a garage in Buffalo.
—George Carlin (1937–2008)

Contents

Acknowledgments

Special thanks to *Buffalo News* sports columnist Mike Harrington, who patiently explained why it's wrong to say "a runhome" and "a downtouch." And to John Koerner, author of *The Father Baker Code*; Jonathan L. White, a Frank Lloyd Wright enthusiast and senior interpretive guide at Forest Lawn Cemetery; and Janice Burnett, Patrick Kavanagh, and Sandra Starks at Forest Lawn Cemetery. Ongoing gratitude to the staff and volunteers at the Buffalo and Erie County Public Library and the Buffalo and Erie County Historical Society for their assistance and all the good work that they do. Much appreciation and a big bucket of wings to all the talented, kind, smart, and helpful folk at Fulcrum Publishing who made both Buffalo books possible, including the supportive and perspicacious publishers Sam Scinta (Sweet Home Class of '87!) and Derek Lawrence, editor extraordinaire Carolyn Sobczak, ingenious and resourceful marketing superwomen Erin Groce and Katie Wensuc, and crackerjack designer Jack Lenzo. A big shout-out to the high priestess of skiing fast and Western New York public relations, Martha Buyer. Thanks to Peter Heffley for his willingness to share an especially difficult chapter in his family's history. Kudos to my mother, Ellen Pedersen, a.k.a. Eagle-Eye Ellen, who has been the proofreader of last resort for all of my work, except those attendance notes I forged in high school. And many thanks to my husband, Willie Pietersen, for his constant encouragement and eternal patience. As for outstanding office manager Aimee Chu, what would we do without you?

No buffalo were harmed during the writing, editing, and printing of this book.

Introduction

*B*uffalo Gal is a memoir I wrote about growing up in Western New York, the title taken from an American folk song with the chorus "Buffalo gals, won't you come out tonight and dance by the light of the moon." It was quickly brought to my attention that most historians believe "Buffalo gals" were prostitutes. However, in my purple snorkel jacket lined with neon orange nylon, black cap with Piglet earflaps, and silver moon boots, I'm certain that I appeared more serial killer chic than streetwalker.

The action took place during the fiscally forlorn stagflation seventies, featuring the decline of manufacturing, an unpopular war in Vietnam, the biggest recession since the Great Depression, and an energy crisis. As the home of Big Steel, the Buffalo area was hit exceptionally hard. And along with being a flash point for antiwar demonstrations, race riots, and pro-life rallies, it was a place where energy was particularly coveted, especially in the form of heat during the winter months. Money was so tight that working-class people didn't stamp their phone and electric bills, and nary a one ever came back. The only heated toilet seats were in the homes of large families, where an endless line of crosslegged customers impatiently waited to sit on them, which is thought to be the root of Irish step dancing, and if the queue didn't move quickly enough, you ended up with a variety called Riverdance. This is slightly different from the Lego Dance, which erupted whenever parents stepped on a stray Lego piece in bare feet and skipped around hollering that someone was "going to see the back of a hand."

Santa Claus was kind of a cruel story to tell Western New York children when I was growing up in the seventies.

You could ask for a pony or a motorbike all you wanted, but no matter how good you'd been, you weren't going to get it. In retrospect, the Santa situation must have dealt just as hard a blow to parents. With every new round of layoffs, dreams of their children having a better life were dying in ditches like so many fairground fish. They could promise a white Christmas and not a lot more. Harmonica-toting blues singers with writer's block headed to Buffalo from all over the country for inspiration, while natives packed up for good as entire neighborhoods became synonymous with drugs, gangs, graffiti, crime, and prostitution. The snowplows wouldn't even go down certain streets, leaving residents to fend for themselves in the scariest driver's ed movie ever made. The city was in its late Elvis period—deteriorating, self-destructive, barely hanging on, and swiftly losing fans.

While completing *Buffalo Gal*, I was struck by how much things had improved in the Buffalo area and decided that having covered The Fall, and despite an overwhelming urge to add to the sixteen thousand–plus tomes on Honest Abe by scribing *Lincoln: A Car for All Seasons* or *A Penny for His Thoughts*, my next volume would be about The Rise, or rather, The Resurrection. Plus, it would be something to fill the time while waiting for my dream job as the stage manager at a Samuel Beckett festival.

Buffalo was the nation's eighth largest city in 1900, poised to overtake Chicago. Millionaires twirled their canes and sashayed past elegant mansions on Delaware Avenue, making their way to the exclusive Buffalo Club while their white-gloved wives rode in carriages to the Twentieth Century Club. There'd even been a locally manufactured automobile called The Buffalo back in 1901. It was a light, tiller-steered runabout that came in both gas and electric. Either ahead of its time, behind its time, or just a very bad name for a car, The Buffalo lasted all of a year. By the sixties, "progress" had translated into steel and auto manufacturing moving abroad, while the Saint Lawrence Seaway, railroads, and highways siphoned commercial traffic off the Erie Canal, and well-heeled families fled to the suburbs.

However, by the beginning of 2008, it seemed that Buffalo was once again on the verge of becoming a thriving metropolis, only instead of grain and steel, the businesses at hand were now healthcare, banking, education, and technology, and Buffalo enjoyed all the cultural benefits of a top-tier city with no rush hour. The National Civic League had given the area one of ten All-America City awards in 1996 and again in 2002. *Reader's Digest* had named Buffalo the third cleanest US city environmentally in 2005, a huge achievement in view of the fact that Lake Erie was declared DOA in the sixties and seventies (if you don't include spontaneous combustion), nearby Love Canal had been designated the nation's first Superfund toxic cleanup site in the eighties, and parts of the botanical gardens had to be rebuilt several times because of acid rain.

Preservationists were winning out over demolition crews. "Buffalo could eventually offer a blueprint for repairing America's other shrinking postindustrial cities," wrote Nicolai Ouroussoff in a lengthy Sunday *New York Times* story titled "Saving Buffalo's Untold Beauty" in the fall of 2008.

Friends from high school who'd moved away in the eighties because of the lack of opportunity talked excitedly about returning home. They missed the small-town friendliness, and it wasn't nostalgia for a past that no longer existed. Buffalo has long held the well-deserved nickname City of Good Neighbors. It might be hard to quantify warmth and sociability, but *USA Today* named Buffalo the nation's number one City with a Heart in 2001 (a tribute to midwestern hospitality or else a nod to Buffalonian Wilson Greatbatch, coinventor of the pacemaker). It was the nation's friendliest city, according to readers from more than 120 cities who'd responded by declaring Buffalo the place for which its residents felt the most affection.

Then there's the downstate prying-eyes brain drain. It's been well established that savvy high school grads from Long Island choose Buffalo for college not because these local schools have outstanding reputations, which they do, but because they're as far away as one can get from helicopter parents while still enjoying in-state tuition and quality pizza. However, students who come for college are finding the area is a place where they want to live and work after completing their degrees.

The West Side of Buffalo, renamed Elmwood Village, was voted one of the ten greatest places to live by the American Planning Association in 2007. And *New York* magazine ran a lengthy article in August of 2008 about young professionals moving from New York City to Buffalo for a better quality of life. The diaspora had ended! Indeed, a reverse migration was in effect.

Black Is the New Black

As a result of being born in 1965 in blue-collar Buffalo, New York, that polestar of the Rust Belt constellation, I seem to have missed the golden age of everything—ancient Greece, Pax Romana, Spanish sonnets, the Hollywood musical, air travel, and even the ozone layer. Instead, I've been part and parcel of the shock-and-outrage age of high gas prices, global warming, death by trans fat, and nationwide bankruptcy.

On September 29, 2008, the day that *Buffalo Gal* arrived in stores, the Dow Jones average dropped 778.68, the largest point drop in history, placing the country firmly in the grips of the Great Recession. We were also in the midst of another energy crisis, gas having recently hit an all-time peak of $4.11 a gallon, with prices at Western New York pumps the highest in the nation. Buffalo appeared in the top ten of the *Forbes* list of America's Fastest-Dying Cities. We were five years into an increasingly unpopular and unwinnable war in Iraq and seven years into what appeared to be a costly but futile hunt for terrorists in Afghanistan. Had I jinxed us? Were Afros, sideburns, bell-bottoms, disco, and Toni home perms lurking around the corner?

The Buffalo Bills, who'd made it clear early in the season that they wouldn't be fitted for Super Bowl rings, weren't exactly raising morale in the fall of 2008. As the team lost to the New York Jets, the game was interrupted by breaking news of then president George W. Bush ducking shoes lobbed at him during a press conference in Iraq, and compared to the Buffalo players on the field, Bush looked positively agile. In fact, putting on a Bills game had suddenly become a way to empty out a bar, much the same way my grandfather used to do by singing World War I songs (all verses) in Tommy Martin's speakeasy at 12 1/2 Seneca Street.

President George W. Bush went from lame duck to dead duck as Congress passed a $700 billion package to rescue the nation's banks from the worst financial crisis since the 1930s. Or, as my seventy-seven-year-old father put it, "Mark Twain came in with Halley's Comet and went out with it, so I guess I came in with the Great Depression and will go out with that." The Emergency Economic Stabilization Act of 2008, more commonly known as the Bailout, was unpopular with the public, who by and large felt they were being flimflammed once again by the same people who'd brought them the hypercapitalism of no-money-down mortgages with adjustable rates that had been adjusted upward, and credit cards that started with no or low interest rates and promptly skyrocketed until they reached debt collection agencies. The government that gave us Operation Enduring Freedom (which sounded more like a new type of birth control or maxi pad), Operation Spartan Scorpion, and Operation O.K. Corral might have considered tagging their "bailout" package with a catchier name, such as Operation Rip-Roaring Rescue and Reinvestment.

Our very first MBA president (Harvard, no less) oversaw a budget death spiral that went from a $236 billion surplus to a $500 billion deficit. Obviously the thinking here was, "This is money that we owe ourselves so let's just forget about it." Remember your parents constantly scolding, "Money doesn't grow on trees!" Actually, it turns out that it does. Money is a paper product, just like toilet tissue, and so long as there are forests, we can just print some more, regular or two-ply.

With the bailout in place, the Dow continued to plunge below 7,000, more than 50 percent below its high of over 14,000 just a year earlier. Several apocalyptic Ponzi schemes were uncovered, including those operated by Richard Piccoli in Buffalo and Bernie Madoff in Manhattan. Investors quickly turned from stocks, swaps, and bonds to gold, guns, and lifeboats. Easter 2009 brought a nationwide nest-egg hunt, with the Dow having just touched its lowest level in over a decade. Unemployment hit a twenty-five-year high of 8.5 percent and was on the way up. In the Buffalo area, the official rate was 9.6 percent (though considerably higher when calculated under broader definitions including those who have given up looking for work) and was much worse for minorities. Even with its first African American mayor, Byron Brown, on the job since 2006, Buffalo still had one of the highest black male jobless rates in the country. And nearly 30 percent of the city's population was officially classified as poor, making Buffalo the nation's third poorest city, behind Detroit and then Cleveland (whose sassy boosters proudly claim, "We're not Detroit!").

On November 4, 2008, the American people elected Barack Hussein Obama as their new president and in the process left many encouraged, believing the country had finally overcome a sad and sordid past of slavery and segregation. The most common sentiment I heard in downtown Buffalo on election night was, "I wish my [mother, father, brother, grandmother, fill in the blank] had lived to see this!"

In January of 2009 the first black family moved into 1600 Pennsylvania Avenue, a house built partly by slaves, 148 years after the Civil War began. Countless African Americans hadn't even been able to cast their ballot until President Lyndon B. Johnson signed into law the Voting Rights Act of 1965, just a few months after civil rights activist Viola Liuzzo was murdered in cold blood by the Ku Klux Klan for giving blacks a ride home in her station wagon after a march in Selma, Alabama. I don't remember that since it was the year I was born, but I clearly recall attending elementary school in the early seventies and having a crayon in my box called "flesh" that was pale peach.

The nationwide financial downturn, compounded by the ongoing machinations of a corrupt and dysfunctional New York State legislature, had taken the high hopes for a Western New York renaissance down along with it. As many of us vividly recalled from the Long-suffering Seventies, Buffalonians continued to experience the aftershocks of that recession for years, while most of the country was well on the road to recovery. But this time there were a few signs that things might turn out differently. And I don't mean the big green signs that say Peace Bridge to Canada Next Right.

I've Got the World on a String Theory

In February of 2009, I was forced to cancel my long-standing subscription to *Forbes* magazine when it ranked Buffalo eighth on a list of America's Ten Most Miserable Cities (and then repeated the insult in 2010). This was not an action I took lightly, since a family friend's cast-off copies of *Forbes* had taught me everything I knew about business. At age eighteen I even wrote to publisher Malcolm Forbes and told him that, unable to find opportunity in my hometown in 1983, I was off to seek my fortune on Wall Street based on all that I'd gleaned from the glossy pages of his magazine. The Manhattan-wise brokers and clerks on the dog-eat-dog trading floor ate naive girls like me for breakfast, and I fell for their practical jokes—frantically running from post to post and finally to the chairman's office in search of a bag of upticks, their version of the left-handed monkey wrench. But all that changed the day Malcolm Forbes's reply came addressed to me at the stock exchange. The guys were stunned to see an embossed envelope from the publisher of *Forbes* and immediately wanted to know how I might be related to or acquainted with the legendary mogul. I tucked the envelope into my pocket as if Malc and I had been best friends forever. Later I discovered it contained only a pleasant form letter, but I was never again sent for the odd-lot stretcher or the keys to the clearinghouse or a bacon double cheeseburger at the kosher deli (which I *didn't* fall for, since my godparents were Jewish).

Still, after three decades of periodical bliss and mutual respect, it was the end of a beautiful capitalist friendship with *Forbes*, and I hope the new publisher understands why. Their Misery Measure took into account commute times, corruption, pro sports teams, Superfund sites, income tax, sales tax, unemployment, violent crime, and weather. Why didn't it include art, architecture, and culture, areas in which Buffalo shines, from highbrow to pierced brow, with its many galleries, theaters, architectural treasures, museums, and restaurants? Superstar chef Anthony Bourdain stopped to sample the fare and declared the city not only "beautiful, especially in winter," but "a sentimental favorite," and in 2009 *Esquire* magazine rated homegrown Ted's Hot Dogs and Mighty Taco two of the best fast-food chains in America. And I'll take the liberty of adding stand-alone Saigon Bangkok, Risa's, Le Metro, Brodo, and Papaya.

Buffalo, which ranked between Detroit and Miami among *Forbes*'s Les Misérables, was taken to task for its surplus snowfall and incredible shrinking population (which peaked at 618,000 in 1960 and is now about 270,000). And why is Buffalo snow a problem? Many cities ranked as the best places to live have plenty of snow. The white stuff seems to be fine in Fargo, no problem in Nashua, boffo in Boise, and perfect in Provo. Paintings by Norman Rockwell and Grandma Moses feature snow. I wasn't aware there was good snow and bad snow, aside from newly fallen snow and yellow snow. Why didn't they take into account that the National Weather Service has never recorded the mercury as being over 100 degrees in this city with such perfect summers? Frostbite, maybe a little. Heatstroke, not a chance.

We're talking about a city with an infrastructure designed to support many more people than its current population, and as a result there are few lines and even fewer traffic jams. You needn't arrive at beaches at the butt crack of dawn to get a good spot, and you don't see smackdowns over picnic tables in the parks. Citizens rest easy knowing there won't be any shortage of hospital beds if the Chicken Wing Flu strikes.

Still, no one I knew felt miserable when *Forbes* so unexpectedly lashed out at us. However, the following week a local Muslim man decapitated his wife because she was divorcing him (he'd already been divorced twice)—a so-called honor killing by a man who, with his wife, was running a TV station aimed at counteracting negative stereotypes about Muslims. The Unitarian Women's Group (less a sewing circle and more a tactical team against injustice) hadn't been so berserk since 2002, when a Nigerian woman was sentenced to be stoned to death for bearing a child out of wedlock. And before that, when *Little Women* author Louisa May Alcott was told by a well-known Boston publisher, "Stick to your teaching, Miss Alcott. You can't write."

That same night, a plane crashed in the town of Clarence, fourteen miles northeast of Buffalo, killing fifty people. It was a preventable tragedy, the result of a poorly skilled and inadequately trained pilot. Suddenly everyone felt miserable. In an area with over a million people, it's hard to imagine all the threads connecting our lives into one big tapestry, but they're there. Most people had some link to the crash that suddenly made daily existence more tenuous. Mine was that I'd gone to church with the couple to whose home a woman and her daughter fled after their house had been hit by the falling plane, which killed the husband.

Thus, the narrative of my book shifted slightly. It was not a time for new beginnings so much as for belt-tightening and recuperation, and who better at budgeting and refurbishing a torn psyche than Buffalonians? In the classic economic model of scarcity and abundance, Buffalonians have excelled at coupon clipping and dollar stretching over the past half century. Or, as the burglars like to say, we take things as we find them, even Canadian castoffs in mall parking lots, thereby adding a whole new dimension to the phrase *duty-free shopping*. With a history of economic adversity and our legacy as one of the country's most blizzard-beaten areas, when it comes time to hunker down and pray for daylight while remaining cheerful and practical, the nation turns its desperate gaze to us. We've internalized the lines from Samuel Beckett's *Waiting for Godot*: "We wait till we can get up. Then we go on. On!" Or possibly the words of my favorite camp counselor: "Cry all you want. You'll have to pee less."

Western New Yorkers can find the upside to a downward spiral. Surely it's no accident that composer Harold Arlen (1905–1986) was born and raised in Buffalo. In 1929, the year of the stock market crash, he wrote the music for his first best-selling song, "Get Happy." During the depths of the Great Depression, he composed "I've Got the World on a String" (*Life's a wonderful thing!*) and the classic ballad "Over the Rainbow," and following World War II, "Ac-Cent-Tchu-Ate the Positive" and "Come Rain or Come Shine" (*Days may be cloudy or sunny, we're in or we're out of the money, but I'll love you always, I'm with you rain or shine*).

We're a stoic people and the champions of waiting it out, whether it's for the Super Bowl, the Stanley Cup, or spring. Pray for sun, prepare for rain. If Buffalo had been around in biblical times, we'd have continued about our business through plague and pestilence. Frogs—wear boots. Hail—how about ice cream? Grasshoppers—perfect for a frozen blended afternoon cocktail. Indeed, Hang in There cat posters and Keep on Truckin' mud flaps were made for us.

Just between you and me, archaeologists and bisonologists are quite certain that no buffalo ever roamed Western New York. But there were and still are thousands of industrious beavers building homes and having families. Indeed, the winged beaver might make a better mascot for the area since Buffalonians just keep toiling away until they eventually rise up.

Buffalo is nicknamed the Queen City because it's the second largest city in the state, after New York, or else because at one time it was the second largest city on the Great Lakes, after Chicago. However, any chess player will tell you that it's better to be the queen. The king just stands there while the queen gets all the good moves.

The United States of Iroquois

Prior to middle school, when most major life decisions were made by employing the Magic 8 Ball, the similarly exacting eeny, meenie, miny, mo was used to determine who would go first on a double-dog dare and that sort of thing. However, it was absolutely necessary when dividing up for a game of cowboys and Indians since it was much cooler to be an Indian—not just because of the face paint and war whoops, but because it was only a game, and therefore you could fight hard without ending up conquered when dinner was ready and playtime was over. I guess nowadays kids play cowpersons and indigenous Americans. Or, more likely, computer war games.

In elementary school, we had to write an illustrated report on the Seneca Indian longhouse. The Seneca preferred this big house over groupings of smaller tepees, a wise choice in a Western New York winter and one that has withstood the test of time, as I do not recall ever going to anyone's tepee to play after school. A dozen or so people residing in one dwelling would probably appear crowded to schoolchildren in other parts of the country, but in heavily Catholic Buffalo this was a very common arrangement.

My hometown of Amherst, New York, a few miles northeast of Buffalo, is unusual in that it's named after British Army officer Jeffery Amherst. Many of the surrounding towns have Indian words for names—Cheektowaga, Lackawanna, Tonawanda, West Seneca, Gowanda, and Chautauqua. We also have Scajaquada Creek and the Scajaquada Expressway, which are not impossible to pronounce so long as you don't live near the Sagtikos State Parkway on Long Island, as my grandfather did. If you add in the name of

Native American guide and interpreter Sacajawea, then you must pick two to say, since no person can pronounce Scaja-quada, Sagtikos, *and* Sacajawea.

In addition to tax-free gas and cigarettes, we have the Indians to thank for squash, peanuts, maple sugar, syrup, Thanksgiving, the toboggan, lacrosse, the expression *to bury the hatchet*, and succotash—a stew made of corn, lima beans, and tomatoes. An Indian named Straight Back was invited to dinner by a white pioneer and the meal was served in courses. So when Straight Back invited the pioneer to his place, he also served dinner in courses—succotash, succo-tash, and then succotash. Perhaps that's why the cartoon character Sylvester the Cat used to say, "Suffering succotash."

As a matter of interest, the Iroquois did not own and operate the local Iroquois Brewery. Started as the Jacob Roos Brewery in 1830, Iroquois went on to become the largest brewery in Buffalo and collapsed under financial pressure in 1971. There was no bailout.

Four-fifths of New York State, from the Saint Lawrence River and Adirondack Mountains to Lake Erie and Ohio, had been settled by the original five nations of the Iroquois League (Cayuga, Oneida, Mohawk, Seneca, and Onondaga) at least five hundred years before European settlers started arriving in the sixteenth century. The area around Lake Erie, which shares its latitude with Barcelona and Rome, was particularly popular because of the fertile farmland and good fishing.

The Iroquois have been called the Romans of the New World for the large expanse of territory they amassed through a series of battles. The Beaver Wars, mid-seventeenth-century hostilities over the fur trade between the Iroquois and the Algonquin of the Great Lakes region, were some of the most brutal and bloodiest ever fought in North America. But then the Iroquois formed a constitution, complete with representa-tive democracy, clear divisions between levels of government, and the assurance of free speech. Additionally, they operated a successful league of nations, a vehicle for diplomatically dealing with troublesome tribes, hundreds of years before President Woodrow Wilson called for one in 1918. However, the Iroquois didn't employ a written language, and thus the structure of their organization had to be passed down orally from generation to generation. So basically, if you were skilled at memorizing lengthy tracts or wanted to get out of hunting, that 75,000-word gig was yours for the asking.

This Great Law of Words mapped out by the Iroquois was symbolized by a totem pole topped with a bald eagle, and both would be borrowed by European settlers when they declared independence from England. Still, as we'd later see with the US Constitution and the Civil War, just because they'd written some ground rules for getting along doesn't mean the Iroquois didn't have anger management problems or a monopoly on conflict resolution. For instance, they wiped the Erie Indians clear off the map.

The Iroquois Confederacy (joined by the Tuscarora in 1722) attempted to remain neutral during the American Revolution, but like most neighbors when there's a big ugly divorce, they eventually had to take sides. Four of the six Iroquois Nations fought with the British, while the Oneida and Tuscarora pledged their loyalty to the colonists. In 1779, George Washington, commander of the American forces, sent Major General John Sullivan on a scorched-earth campaign to defeat the Iroquois once and for all. His expedition moved through Central and Western New York, burning Iroquois communities and destroying their crops and orchards. It was one of the most expensive campaigns of the Revolutionary War, using a million dollars from already depleted colonial coffers and employing five thousand soldiers. Refugees fled to Fort Niagara in Youngstown, New York, thirty miles north of Buffalo, where they spent the following winter hungry and miserable. Most Iroquois permanently lost their land, hundreds died of exposure and disease, and many moved to Canada.

In 1797, the Indians sold Western New York, all but 200,000 acres of reservation land, to white agents for $100,000. Some tribes still have outstanding claims over land that was snatched up at the time of the American Revolution or through illegal treaties during the two decades that followed.

In 2004, a mere eight hundred years after the fact, the US government finally acknowledged the influence of the Iroquois Nations' political union and democratic government on the Articles of Confederation and the US Constitution. "[The Iroquois Confederacy] is in fact the oldest democracy on this continent. Its political system, which includes a voice for all and a balance of power between the sexes, existed when Europe still believed in the divine right of kings," says *Stolen Continents* author Ronald Wright.

One substantial difference in the Iroquois government was the inclusion of women, a group that the framers of the US *and* Canadian constitutions bypassed. In fact, under the Iroquois system, women owned the land (or were the designated caretakers, since Native Americans were more into stewardship than ownership), while the men protected it. The chiefs and decision makers were men, but the women selected members for the Grand Council of Chiefs, and if any leader was found veering off course from the Great Law, the Clan Mothers could give him the moccasin.

More recently, the Seneca Nation has built a billion-dollar economy on gas, cigarettes, gambling, and bingo that employs 6,300 taxpaying workers. They're the fourth-largest employer in Western New York, ahead of HSBC, M&T, Catholic Health System, and Tops Markets. So listen to your mother.

Buffalo Burning

I just turned forty, sixty-two months ago, and back when I was growing up we went on a lot of class field trips, since it was a time before skyrocketing insurance rates, a more litigious society, and increased standardized testing. The trips were usually to the Niagara Falls hydroelectric power plant; Tifft Nature Preserve in Buffalo; the Ontario Science Center; Old Fort Niagara in Youngstown, New York; and Fort George in Canada. The last two destinations usually meant a cold, gray, damp day spent tramping through cold, gray, damp stone structures, but we loved not being in the cold, gray, damp classroom (during the dark, dank days of the energy crisis, the school thermostat was locked into place at Wear Several Sweaters, while the lights were permanently affixed at Sit Near a Window). Most of us behaved, especially if our teacher Mr. Leslie was along. Mr. Leslie never yelled at anyone, never sent a child down to the principal, and never phoned anyone's parents. That's because he had few discipline problems as a result of The Thump. A short, smiling, heavyset man, Mr. Leslie would take his thumb and index finger and thwack a mischief maker on the head with a force so strong it could launch a child's cerebellum directly into his frontal lobe. But the true brilliance of The Thump lay in the fact that The Thumper (who should be played by Robert Duvall in the movie version) didn't necessarily let The Thumpee know he'd been caught doing something wrong, thus leading to a false sense of security that The Thumpee had escaped, or else the terror that a mind-numbing Thump was lurking around the corner, because The Thump could come at anytime, anywhere. A shout would suddenly ring out, and we knew that justice had been served and the rest of us should take warning.

Thumps aside, Mr. Leslie was everyone's favorite teacher because he was in charge of ordering movies for our school. He showed lots of educational films featuring avalanches and volcanoes and then played the horrifying parts backward and forward dozens of times. This was before computer-generated special effects, so an avalanche in reverse with people becoming unburied alive and catapulting upward had the same impact on us as when *Star Wars* arrived a few years later. We kids went wild, heaving with laughter and screaming, "Do it again!" Retainers were swallowed. Lunches were lost.

Old Fort Niagara was part of some major Western New York history going all the way back to 1678. Originally a French fortification, it fell after a nineteen-day siege of British redcoats, American colonists, and Native American warriors during the Battle of Fort Niagara in July of 1759. This was an important turning point in the French and Indian War, and had the Brits not prevailed we'd all be drinking Perrier and taking the entire month of August off as paid vacation.

Fort George sprang up in 1802 as headquarters for the British Army in Canada and would be the setting for several significant battles in the War of 1812, also known as The War I Always Have to Look Up. Basically, the United States landed in the middle of a squabble between France and England, we got jiggy and tried to invade Canada, we were repelled, the British got jiggy and tried to invade us, and the boundaries ended up right back where they were. If you, too, are feeling jiggy, the forts offer special events, including battle reenactments complete with bombardments and military music. However, calling the cavalry on cell phones is not permitted.

Before the war wound down in 1814, the village of Buffalo was burned to the ground. In April of 1813, the Americans had crossed Lake Ontario to York (now Toronto) and torched public buildings. More skirmishes followed. In mid-December of 1813, the Americans burned Newark (now Niagara-on-the-Lake), Ontario, and the British, along with help from some non-peace-pipe-smoking Indians, retaliated on December 30 by incinerating Buffalo. Happy New Year! I'll have that drink now.

Lost were 143 residences, businesses, and churches, with twelve villagers left dead, while in the surrounding countryside 334 houses, barns, and stores were destroyed. The redcoats did such a thorough job in town that only the stone jail, a blacksmith shop, and a cottage remained, the last being purposely spared. Margaret St. John, the Heroine of Buffalo, had refused to move her nine children when the British approached, and their general was impressed by her pluck. The mom of my friend and neighbor Mary Pyne had nine children, so I can explain this situation based on firsthand knowledge. The Pynes went on a family vacation exactly once in thirty years, never to be repeated. Packing for that many kids is truly impossible, and when Mary got pinkeye they had to come back early anyway.

Fortunately, the Buffalo locals of the early nineteenth century had their priorities straight, and Pomeroy's Tavern was the first thing rebuilt. Residents were nothing if not creative and resilient. Not surprisingly, the conflagration spurred demand for the city's earliest brick homes.

The city's first physician, Dr. Cyrenius Chapin, took it upon himself to open the first drugstore, and, after losing a patient, he became the first funeral director. During the War of 1812, he was promoted from colonel to lieutenant colonel while engaged in all sorts of derring-do, and he was the final holdout during the Battle of Buffalo, when the British temporarily drove off the city's American defenders. Next, the ever-entrepreneurial Chapin appointed himself negotiator in chief, but the British rejected his credentials and he ended up as a prisoner of the Crown for nine months. Over the following decade, Chapin helped bring the Erie Canal to Buffalo, organize the first county fair, and found the Medical Society of Erie County, of which he became the first president. Chapin Parkway is named after him.

By 1826, the Buffalo/Black Rock area was back in action, with a population of 8,653 and over a thousand homes, businesses, and breweries. There were four public schools, four newspapers, four houses of worship, at least three times as many brothels, and ten times as many saloons. Still, after seeing dozens of books about the Great Chicago Fire of 1871 and the San Francisco earthquake of 1906, and nary a one about the night they drove old Buffalo down, a person wants to say, "Hey, we got our butts burned too!"

The redcoats were finally gone for good from American soil, leaving behind a yen for baked beans and Shakespearean sonnets, weird spellings of words like *theatre* and *catalogue,* and the urge to name our dogs King and Duke. Had it really been a wise idea to march around the thick woods of Western New York and harass people while dressed in bright scarlet jackets with shiny gold epaulets in the first place? The Americans would continue to make a few lame tries at taking Canada, mostly involving pigs—the Aroostook War of 1838–39 resulted in the death of one pig, and the Pig War of 1859 was triggered by the shooting of a pig.

This final Canadian offensive could only have been hatched by a people of such creativity and imagination to include James Joyce, Oscar Wilde, George Bernard Shaw, poet Brendan Behan, who on his deathbed said to the nun caring for him, "Bless you Sister, may all your sons grow up to be Bishops," and Buffalonian Chauncey Olcott, who wrote and composed "My Wild Irish Rose" and cowrote the lyrics for "When Irish Eyes Are Smiling"; a people who, if three are put in a pub together, will somehow end up with four political parties. In 1866, an Irish nationalist organization called the Fenians decided it'd be a grand idea to use Buffalo as a base to attack British targets in Canada and thereby persuade the British to withdraw from Ireland. It brings to mind the definition of Irish Alzheimer's: you only remember the grudges, which is not to be confused with Irish amnesia, where you only forget the food. Ironically, though the raids didn't do much for Irish independence, they helped galvanize support for the confederation of Canada and the collective security of nationhood.

Rather than toss tea in a harbor, storm bastilles, or don black berets, Canadians eventually just asked nicely for their independence. After patching together some provinces, territories, and Tim Hortons donut shops, the Canada Act of 1982 severed any lingering legal dependence on the British parliament. However, to be courteous, they left the queen on some of their money and on the nation's Great Seal, even though she doesn't visit as often as she could.

Mo' Better Bagels

You couldn't beat the early nineteenth century for excitement in Western New York. In 1815, New York State purchased Grand Island, a thirty-three-square-mile parcel smack-dab in the middle of the Niagara River between Buffalo and Niagara Falls, from the Iroquois for a thousand dollars on the barrelhead and a yearly fee of five hundred dollars, which is paid every June to this day. However, the Seneca tribe, part of the Iroquois Confederacy, retained hunting rights. In 1993, the Seneca tried to get back the land, which is now home to a population of about nineteen thousand, including the popular indie-alternative-rock band Inlite. Their argument is that Grand Island was taken without the approval of Washington, and this violates the Trade and Intercourse Act of 1790, which states that Native American lands can't be sold without consent of the federal government. Through a series of court decisions in 2002, 2004, and 2006, the Seneca Nation lost their case.

Okay, this is really not a joke. In 1824, playwright, soldier, impresario, and utopian Mordecai Manuel Noah acquired two thousand acres on Grand Island to found a Jewish homeland. It was to be called Ararat, after Mount Ararat (in what's now Turkey), the biblical resting place of Noah's Ark, and if it succeeded could've potentially saved us from the tasteless frozen bagels of the 1960s and '70s, which easily doubled as hockey pucks.

Noah believed that some of the Native Americans were from the Lost Tribes of Israel, and it's possible his ideas influenced Joseph Smith, who founded the Latter-day Saint movement (a.k.a. the Mormon Church) a few years later. Noah was convinced that the Jews needed to return and rebuild

31

their ancient homeland on Grand Island. However, the idea didn't fly, and bad weather kept Noah from even making it to the dedication ceremony. Furthermore, I'm not sure if there's a single synagogue on Grand Island today, though it'd be hard to find anyhow between the lawn statues of angels and Blessed Virgin Marys, or if you're there around Eastertide, the warren of thirty-foot-high inflatable rabbits. And a recent swingers convention at the local Holiday Inn brought out plenty of pastors. In protest.

However, Grand Island is home to Martin's Fantasy Island amusement park, which prides itself on being welcoming, safe, fun, and affordable. And even if most of the locals don't throw Purim parties, many of us fondly remember the "Fun! Wow!" commercials of the 1970s. Men who were teens during that era of the shoulderless, sleeveless tube top, a.k.a boob tube, surely remember strategically positioning themselves where the Wild Mouse ride took its sharpest turn and often caused the cups of well-endowed women to runneth over.

As the Seneca lands were taken and they began leaving the Buffalo River settlement during the mid-1800s, a religious sect from Germany established the Ebenezer Community of True Inspiration, formally adopted communism, and developed a network of six villages with jointly owned mills, factories, and farms. However, as a friend from West Berlin once explained to me about East Germany in the 1970s, "Communism will never succeed because you cannot keep a German from working." Similarly, in 1855 the Community of True Inspiration relocated to Iowa and went on to form a joint stock company for the purpose of manufacturing and selling Amana kitchen appliances. What started with a belief in mysticism and Pietism ended in the side-by-side refrigerator/freezer. And thank God for that.

Leave It to the Beavers

While people grow up singing "Dixie" down South and "(I've Got Spurs That) Jingle Jangle Jingle" out West, in New York State it's "Fifteen Miles on the Erie Canal" (a.k.a. "Low Bridge, Everybody Down"). Ask any Buffalonian to fill in the blank: "I've got an old mule and her name is ___" (rhymes with *Hal* but starts with an *S*). This ditty was a staple in the repertoire of our elementary school music teacher, who similarly favored the French Canadian folk song "Alouette." I subsequently discovered the latter was about tearing the feathers off the head of a beautiful skylark being prepared for the oven, and this song, in conjunction with my employment on a farm, was the reason I became a vegetarian. It was similarly traumatic to be told that "Ring around the Rosie" (or, if you were Catholic, "Ring around the Rosary") was actually about the bubonic plague, and that's why at the end "We all fall down!"

The creation of the Erie Canal reads much like an O. Henry story, known for their great characterizations and surprise endings. Flour merchant Jesse Hawley went to debtor's prison in 1807 after he lost money because of the poor roadways available to move his goods. From his jail cell, writing under the heroic name Hercules, Hawley published more than a dozen essays on the prospect of a canal from the Hudson River to Lake Erie. Many said they were the ravings of a lunatic; however, a few prominent men, including future governor DeWitt Clinton, saw the seeds of genius.

George Washington, prior to becoming president, was in favor of a different gateway to the West—a canal from the Potomac River, on which he was coincidentally the largest property owner. In 1784, the enterprising father of our country raised funds for a private company to undertake his own project, which eventually collapsed. It was one of the few instances in history where a federally financed venture, in this case the Erie Canal, would manage to outperform entrepreneurship, even if it was judged to be an enormous boondoggle along the way.

Joseph Ellicott (1760–1826), who had laid out the city of Buffalo, fought for the Erie Canal's western terminus to be in Buffalo and not the Black Rock area to the northwest, which had a more protected harbor. He succeeded. (Don't feel bad, because 120 years later Black Rock would get Rich Products, and if you've ever had their éclairs or mousse cakes you know what I'm talking about.) However, Ellicott was plagued by depression, and family members sent him to Bellevue Hospital in New York City, where he hanged himself in 1826.

Still, Joseph Ellicott is to Western New York what John and Robert Kennedy are to the rest of the country. His name is on two towns, a village, a square, a building, a street, a dormitory, a creek, a park, a road, and an elementary school. A bridge and a Ben & Jerry's ice cream flavor are surely not far behind.

At least these names have a provenance, whereas the person who went berserk with the words *maple* (Maple Road, Maplemere, Maplewood, Maple West—eh, are we in Canada?) and *beaver* (Beaver Island, Beaver Meadow, Beaver Lake, Beaver Hollow) was just plain unimaginative. I guess it could be worse. In Manhattan, there's a neighborhood called Turtle Bay, which is home to neither bay nor turtle, at least of the free-ranging or nonchocolate varieties.

Another song, "Erie Canal," sheds considerably more light on the times with the chorus "Oh, the E-ri-e is a risin', and the gin is gettin' low, and I scarcely think we'll get a drink 'till we get to Buffalo-oh-oh." More than three thousand Irish laborers were employed on this early mass transit project. And to get work on the canal done quickly, there was an incentive plan—casks of whiskey placed along the Buffalo stretch for intrepid workers to find. Meantime, two oxen drivers named their animals Jesus Christ and God Almighty so they could swear with impunity up and down the canal.

Finally, on October 26, 1825, Governor DeWitt Clinton started a ten-day inaugural journey along the 365-mile Erie Canal, which now connected Lake Erie to the Hudson River. Clinton brought with him two barrels of water from Lake Erie and upon arriving in New York City poured the contents into the Atlantic, kicking off a hundred years of prosperity for Buffalo and other towns along the artificial waterway and transforming New York into the Empire State. Travel time for passengers and cargo went from two months in a bumpy wagon to ten days on a smooth canal boat. The cost of shipping a ton of goods from Albany to Buffalo dropped from one hundred dollars to ten dollars, and enough tolls were collected so that the canal turned a profit just ten years after opening. A seemingly impossible undertaking known as "Clinton's Folly" or "Clinton's Ditch" was quickly relabeled "The Eighth Wonder of the World" and is still considered to be one of the greatest engineering marvels of modern times.

Buffalo grew along the banks of Lake Erie while handling massive shipments of grain and other raw materials sent from the Rockies and the Midwest to the growing eastern seaboard and on to Europe. While making New York City the nation's richest port, the canal brought a surge in population and commerce, which led Buffalo to incorporate as a city in 1832 with about ten thousand people. Back then, cockfights were permitted but were called "chicken disputes." (Obviously the historical dotted line to the Korean War's billing as a "conflict" and Vietnam being labeled a "police action.") However, the city charter forbade prostitution, billiards, card playing, and that ultimate vice, bowling. As it turned out, aside from tracking the sound of wooden pins being hit, these rules were difficult to enforce. Canal Street alone boasted over a hundred bars and brothels, earning the nickname "The Wickedest Street in the World," which is so much catchier than "You've got a friend in Pennsylvania" or "Oklahoma is OK."

Living in Buffalo during the 1970s, it was sad to look back at a time when canal traffic was heavy and the city was a thriving center of industry, the western outpost of the East and the East's gateway to the West. But the famed area is experiencing a rebirth. The Erie Canal Harbor in downtown Buffalo, the historic western terminus, now has a naval and military park complete with ships that can be toured, including the USS *The Sullivans*. *The Sullivans* was the first American navy ship to be named after more than one person. The five Sullivan brothers from Waterloo, Iowa, all enlisted on January 3, 1942, under the condition that they serve together; they perished together on November 13, 1942, when the USS *Juneau* sank after being hit by a torpedo during the Battle of Guadalcanal.

In addition to the park, there's also an aerospace museum and plans for small businesses in canal-era-style buildings laid out on the original street grid. Only, watch out kids, because there are so many informational placards and interpretive signs that the place just screams educational field trip. If you suddenly feel a skull-shattering thump or hear the squishy wet sound of a not yet fully formed brain smacking into a hard skull, it's most certainly the ghost of Mr. Leslie.

Likewise, the waterway itself is staging a comeback. Although they weren't pulled by mules, 112 commercial shipments navigated the Erie Canal in 2009, with the number expected to rise as the high price of fuel makes barges a cost-effective alternative to trucks.

A scenic place for plying pleasure craft, the canal also features walking and biking trails. And while stuck on an Amtrak train outside of Chittenango, New York—birthplace of *Wizard of Oz* creator Frank Baum, complete with yellow-brick road, which is now a sidewalk in this age of downsizing—one might decide it's actually *faster* to take a barge on the Erie Canal from Albany to Buffalo. Even one pulled by mules.

Angola Horror

Peter Heffley was my eighth grade social studies teacher at Sweet Home Junior High School. We became lifelong friends after discovering that we both collected bizarre newspaper stories. Our most prized article was titled "Meet Me at the Top of the Hill," in which an outlaw motorcycle gang arrived at their designated meeting point only to crash into one another. It wasn't the tragedies themselves we relished but the resulting headlines, for example, "Deaf Mute Gets New Hearing in Killing," "Farmer Bill Dies in House," and "Headless Body in Topless Bar."

Over the years, Pete has gone from looking like Mahatma Gandhi to Vladimir Lenin, or maybe Vladimir Lenin living in a hollow tree and making cookies. Either way, at this point he's just a black top hat, monocle, and spats away from becoming Mr. Peanut. However, when some Buffalonians were having dinner at a restaurant in the heart of New Delhi, India, discussing Pete, of all things, and a person at the next table said, "Are you talking about Peter Heffley? He was my favorite teacher!" his reputation somehow went international.

Pete's parents always attended the yearly high school musical extravaganza, and that's where I first met them. His mother, Mildred, was a Smith prior to marrying Walter Heffley in 1936, and her parents had owned Smith Drugstore at the corner of Bailey and Kensington. Before that, Grandpa Smith ran a pharmacy on the edge of the Canal District back in the days when cocaine and heroin were basically over-the-counter remedies and folks could nip in for a quick fix on their coffee breaks.

The family name was originally Goldschmidt, but Pete likes to say they put the gold in the bank and kept the

41

Schmidt—until World War I, when that became Smith, just to be on the safe side. Peter was an old family name, just not in Pete's family. Pete's dad, Walter Heffley, was a dead ringer for Kentucky Fried Chicken's Colonel Sanders, especially in his later years, but he was a kind and gentle man who never got angry at anyone for asking if he could swing them a deal on the twelve-piece Big Bucket with mashed potatoes, gravy, and a side of slaw. As a young man, Walter had been a champion boxer, but after hearing the crack of his opponent's head as it hit the gym floor, he could never again enter the ring.

Having ruled out becoming a pugilist, Walter turned to teaching. He began his career in a one-room schoolhouse and eventually became the superintendent of the Cleveland Hill School District. Once, while Walter was eating his favorite dish of half a dozen ears of sweet corn dripping with butter, I asked if it'd been his lifelong dream to become a teacher. "Well," he wiped some butter from his beard, "I was working at Bethlehem Steel and my sister Mary was going to Buffalo State Teachers College and Mother turned to me and said, 'Walt, you go along with her.'" Despite such inauspicious beginnings, Walter was an extremely successful administrator and fondly known around the school district as "Last Chance Heffley." Whether you were pregnant or on probation or had just made some bad choices, he'd help you graduate.

By the time I met them, Pete's parents had retired to Angola Village, on the shore of Lake Erie, twenty-two miles south of Buffalo. The name Angola seems to have been selected in the early 1850s because the locals, primarily Quakers, were supporting missionary efforts in the African country of Angola. The village is known for being the birthplace of famous Buffalonian Willis Carrier (1876–1950), inventor of the air conditioner. It was before cooling technology had led to cryogenics, so Carrier was buried in Buffalo's Forest Lawn Cemetery, along with his three wives, and eventually the family moved the business to Nebraska. However, Carrier left behind a lasting legacy for schoolchildren everywhere with his firm belief that time spent staring into space and just thinking is not wasted.

The economy of Angola improved dramatically with the arrival of a railroad line in 1852. But on December 18, 1867, the Buffalo-bound New York Express of the Lake Shore and Michigan Southern derailed its last coach because of a slightly bent axle combined with a poorly maintained track, and the car plunged forty feet off a truss bridge into Big Sister Creek, just two thousand feet east of Angola Station. The next car was pulled from the track and rolled down the far embankment. Stoves set both coaches on fire, and about fifty passengers were killed (accounts differ slightly). Three people managed to crawl from the wreckage, and forty more were injured as the train traveled some distance before the crew realized an accident had happened. John D. Rockefeller, who would go on to found Standard Oil and become one of the richest men in the world, just missed being on the train. He'd pulled into Cleveland's Union Station a few minutes late that morning, thus his bags were on the train and burned in the wreck but his body wasn't.

One good thing to come out of the disaster was a new nationwide emphasis on safety, according to *Buffalo News* writer Charity Vogel, who is working on a book about the tragedy, called *Angola Horror*, based on her excellent article in *American History* magazine. Rockefeller, the entrepreneurial tycoon who narrowly escaped the Angola wreck, went on to market oil products formulated to ignite at much higher temperatures. As a result, travel by both train and steamboat became much less hazardous.

Meantime, inventor and entrepreneur George Westinghouse Jr., appalled by the catastrophic train wrecks of his day, set his sights on finding a quicker and safer way of stopping railcars in an emergency. The result was the air brake, an invention that revolutionized train travel. By 1893, the federal government made air brakes and automatic couplers mandatory on trains in the United States, a change that reduced the accident rate on the nation's rails by 60 percent.

Similarly, train wreck survivor Benjamin Betts became an engineer and architect who focused on making better bridges. His plans were used to build the first cantilever bridge over the Niagara River and inspired similar designs around the world.

Still, as we recently saw with the 2009 crash of flight 3407 in Clarence Center, which led to some new flight crew rules nationwide, it too often takes a fatal catastrophe to raise safety standards.

Forest to Forest Lawn

There is probably no better testimonial to Buffalo's illustrious past than Forest Lawn Cemetery, which continues to celebrate the people who made the city great. And certainly no place showcases Buffalo's pride and eccentricity as well as Forest Lawn. Savannah's got nothing on us when it comes to being a half bubble off plumb.

Founded in 1849, this 269-acre graveyard is right smack in the middle of the city on what is now some of the most prized and expensive real estate. The cemetery is home to about 156,000 permanent residents, including President Millard Fillmore (1800–1874), who is buried in the family plot, recognizable by a polished red granite obelisk. It lists only his name, date of birth, and date of death, with nothing about him having served as president of the United States. Only a small bronze plaque identifies the grave as belonging to a former commander in chief. Fillmore was equally modest in life, having turned down an honorary degree from Oxford University because it was written in Latin and he firmly believed a person shouldn't accept a degree he couldn't read. While Fillmore was in the White House, the Buffalo city directories continued to count him as a local citizen, listing his occupation as president of the United States and his address not as the White House at 1600 Pennsylvania Avenue, but on Franklin Street in downtown Buffalo.

Diplomatic even in death, Fillmore is buried with both his first and second wives. Abigail, the first Mrs. Fillmore, caught a cold while attending the inauguration of her husband's successor, Franklin Pierce, and died twenty-five days later. Millard Fillmore also gets the Best Friends Forever Award for being buried near his buddies. The obelisk to the east of Fillmore's memorializes Nathan Hall, and the one next to that, Solomon Haven. The three were partners and friends who, in death, remain side by side in the alphabetical order of their law firm's name: Fillmore, Hall, and Haven.

Other famous folks buried in Forest Lawn include Louise Blanchard Bethune (1856–1913), America's first female architect and the designer of Buffalo's Lafayette Hotel, a 367-room redbrick and white terra-cotta French Renaissance–style building considered one of the fifteen finest hotels in America when it opened back in 1904. John Frank Hoover, who was part of the unit that caught President Lincoln's assassin, John Wilkes Booth, also rests in Forest Lawn, along with American explorer Frederick Cook, who claimed to have reached the North Pole in April of 1908, a year before Robert Peary. Unfortunately, Cook had a history of prevarication, falsely professing to have reached the top of Mount McKinley (lesson: always take a photo from the summit). He attempted to win back his reputation in the Texas oil fields, but was imprisoned for mail fraud after sending out flyers saying his discoveries were larger than they actually were. In a note of cosmic irony, Cook's oil wells eventually exceeded his overinflated claims. In another, Robert Peary's claim now appears dubious as well, though he probably got closer to the North Pole than Cook.

Recently added to Forest Lawn is the gravestone of musician Rick James (1948–2004), where devoted followers can pay tribute by singing "Standing on the Top" and "U Bring the Freak Out," leave behind some crack cocaine and bail money, and then go toss back a few shots while listening to a local band named Rick James' Dealer play their rousing song "Make Father Baker a Saint."

When it comes to memorials, the prize for most zany goes to Buffalo's Blocher family. In an architectural school all its own, where Russian Church meets magical mushroom, a sixty-ton bell-shaped granite roof sits atop rectangular columns separated by floor-to-ceiling glass windows. Inside, marble figures of father John Blocher and mother Elizabeth Blocher stand grieving over their dead son, Nelson, while a voluptuous, full-lipped female angel with a come-hither expression gazes down from above.

Is there ever a story behind this one—more like a Puccini opera. Let's start with the hovering Charlie's angel, which is said to bear a striking resemblance to a maid employed by the Blocher family, as well as Botticelli's Venus climbing out of her clamshell. John Blocher was a businessman who'd made a fortune off the idea that shoes could be manufactured in different sizes for the masses rather than custom made. He got married and installed himself on Delaware Avenue, Buffalo's ritziest address. John and Elizabeth's only child, Nelson, was born in 1847, and at age thirty-four was not only a bachelor, but still living at home. In the spring of 1881, the Blochers hired a new maid, Katherine, and son Nelson was instantly love struck. His parents didn't approve of the upstairs boy/downstairs girl match and tried to end the romance by dragging Nelson off on a European tour. When he returned, Katherine had disappeared, leaving behind only her Bible, and poor Nelson was heartbroken. He searched for his true love until he was sick with fever, and on January 24, 1884, he died a miserable man.

John Blocher couldn't find the right artisan to do justice to his family's memorial, so without any training he took up the task himself. For the statues, he hired Paul Roche of Rhode Island to come to Buffalo and carve them out of Carrara marble. But when the first sculpture was unveiled, the hard-to-please Blocher chopped it to pieces with an ax. He then commissioned Swiss-born Italian sculptor Frank Torrey for the job, and it is his work that stands in the cemetery today. The statue of Nelson is clutching a Bible. Even more noticeable is the fact that all the participants are wearing really fine shoes!

The bodies of the three Blochers lie underneath a movable slab in the floor. Hopeless romantics and fans of time-travel movies insist that there's another crypt below the memorial reserved for Katherine, so that Nelson might still spend eternity with her. However, an official at Forest Lawn states with conviction, "No, there are only three crypts," and so it would appear that Nelson is spending eternity with his devoted parents.

Along similar *Masterpiece Theatre* plotlines, the Schickel family monument features four beautifully carved graceful granite figures: an angel, a seated mother with her child, and a life-size female figure. An artistic representation of Mr. Schickel is notably absent, but it would appear that his wife and mistress are peering down disapprovingly at him in his new underground digs, and the angel is regarding him as what detectives might call "a person of interest." This site never fails to remind my friend Russ of his favorite joke about the woman who didn't like her husband very much and didn't want to spend the money on a newspaper obituary after he died. However, the family convinced her it was the right thing to do, and so she submitted, "Martin's dead." The salesperson said that she still had three more words, so she amended it to "Martin's dead. Buick for sale."

Forest Lawn is unusual in that its original mission as a "rural cemetery" was to serve both the dead and the living. As a result, it's not only a place of rest but also a picnicker's paradise, a popular backdrop for wedding photos, and a significant outdoor sculpture museum. The first installation, back in 1851, was a large bronze statue of the Seneca Indian chief Red Jacket (1750–1830). Red Jacket took this name because of a military coat given to him by the British for his wartime services. The Seneca had placed a bad bet by taking the British side during the American Revolution, but they supported the Americans in the War of 1812 by fighting against the British. Thus, Red Jacket is depicted wearing the richly embroidered red jacket presented to him by a British officer, while on his breast is displayed the large medal awarded to him by President George Washington. Red Jacket was a talented orator, and so the Seneca gave him the name Sa-Go-Ye-Wat-Ha (He Who Keeps Them Awake). He had no interest in being converted to Christianity and once told a missionary, "If you white people murdered the Savior, make it up for yourselves. We had nothing to do with it. Had he come among us, we would have treated him better." Instead, Red Jacket suggested that Christianity should first be employed by his white neighbors, and if he saw that they became more honest and less likely to cheat the Indians, then he'd consider it. He was also fond of saying that whites would be happier if they adopted the *Indians'* religion. Cheeky devil.

Red Jacket was a talented drinker and could well have kicked off the first AA meeting with his statement:

> Red Jacket was once a great man, and in favor with the Great Spirit. He was a lofty pine among the smaller trees of the forest. But, after years of glory, he degraded himself by drinking the firewater of the white man. The Great Spirit has looked upon him in anger, and his lightning has stripped the pine of its branches.

Sadly, Red Jacket seems to have been rooked by the white man in death. He was initially buried in a Native American cemetery, but his remains were dug up and moved to Forest Lawn despite his specific wish that no white man reinter him.

Forest Lawn's additional public sculptures and works of art include the Oishei Memorial Bell, eight bronze interacting human figures called "Celebration," an abstract eternal flame, and a sixteen-foot fiberglass angel lifting a human. Private memorials abound, designed by famous architects like Richard Upjohn and Stanford White and the sculptors Augustus Saint Gaudens and Harriet Frishmuth. The largest and most expensive to date is the Letchworth-Skinner mausoleum, an opulent three-level sandstone Greek temple with an interior of Italian and Egyptian marble containing sarcophagi and crypts. Also on the showy side is the Orson Phelps extravaganza by Italian sculptor Nicola Cantalamessa-Papotti, which has five carved marble figures—Faith, Hope, Charity, Fortitude, and the angel Gabriel on top, holding the horn he will supposedly blow one day. You just know that the Phelps family living room furniture was covered in plastic.

My favorite place to sit and contemplate the hereafter is at Mirror Lake, with its Three Graces bronze fountain, while gazing out at the small island, home to a bronze statue of a child. "The Little Girl" was created by Grace Rumsey Goodyear in memory of all children who have died, and almost every day that the weather is nice flowers are placed next to her plaque on shore. However, one must be vigilant with regard to cranky, well-fed, marauding, border-busting Canada geese, which travel in honking packs trying to nip at and intimidate the undead.

The best resting place, and I mean to rest for an hour or so and not eternally, is Chester and Gloria Stachura's place, a white granite mausoleum with heavy bronze doors. Pedestrians can relax on a polished black granite couch or an S-shaped tête-à-tête sofa in front of the entrance. Just bring some newspapers or, better yet, a blanket, because that cold dark granite doesn't get a lot of sun and will freeze your behind. And don't be alarmed if you're awoken by birders with binoculars. There are over 240 varieties of freeloading winged ones ensconced in dozens of rent-controlled bird-houses throughout the cemetery, though they still seem to prefer crapping on the statues.

The winning epitaph at Forest Lawn has to be Amaryl-lis Jones's "I TOLD YOU I WAS SICK," which is not all that different from my husband's upcoming "I HAD THE RIGHT OF WAY," which will be the result of a deadly encounter with a Manhattan bicycle messenger. He insists that he's one of the few people who can claim to know how they will die, but not when.

The cemetery offers terrific tours during the summer months, complete with live actors playing famous but sol-idly deceased historical figures who leap out from behind tombstones and recount highlights from their exciting lives. Unfortunately, the late Geraldine Rudderow does not make a presentation, but the story goes that she had all of her beloved locally made Kittinger furniture loaded into the crypt along with her, and if she *were* to speak, I assume she'd tell us that you can indeed take it with you. Just call U-Haul.

Father Baker's Dozen

Buffalo was historically a Catholic stronghold where every day was Mother's Day, meaning a celebration of the Blessed Virgin Mary, mother of Jesus, Queen of Heaven.

Had there been a movie about Father Nelson Henry Baker, *Boys Town* star Spencer Tracy would've played the lead. Father Baker was a Roman Catholic priest born in Buffalo on February 16, 1842, to a grocer father and a devout Irish Catholic mother. In July of 1863, Baker enlisted to fight in the Civil War as part of the 74th Regiment of the New York State militia. Within days, he found himself fighting for the Union outside Gettysburg, in one of the most violent battles of all time, and was then sent to New York City to help stop the Draft Riots. Back in Buffalo, the twenty-one-year-old Baker considered becoming a priest, but instead opened a successful feed and grain business with a friend.

On September 2, 1869, Baker entered Our Lady of Angels Seminary at Suspension Bridge in Niagara Falls (now Niagara University). Soon he headed for Europe and spent time admiring the Parisian shrine to Our Lady of Victory, a name for the biblical Mary said to have been invoked by early Christians going into battle. Following a brief meeting with Pope Pius IX at the Vatican, he returned home with a renewed sense of faith. Baker was ordained on March 19, 1876 (the feast of Saint Joseph), at the age of thirty-four, and assigned to Limestone Hill (now Lackawanna), just south of Buffalo—a parish that consisted of Saint Patrick's Church, Saint Joseph's Orphanage, and Saint John's Protectory, which provided training and education for at-risk youth. Father Baker labored as an assistant until he was transferred to Saint Mary's Parish in Corning, New York, in 1881. However, he was reassigned to Limestone Hill in 1882 with a promotion to superintendent and wouldn't leave again.

A few days after returning, angry creditors descended on Saint Patrick's, informing Father Baker that the institutions he ran had amassed $56,000 in debt and demanding immediate payment. The business-savvy priest assured everyone they'd receive their money. A predecessor to a modern telemarketer, Father Baker asked postmasters all over the country to obtain the names and addresses of Catholic women, and he wrote for help. Soon, not only were all the creditors paid in full, but the Limestone Hill institutions were looking to expand. On June 26, 1889, a beautiful new chapel and an enlarged protectory were dedicated.

Around the same time, Buffalo was beginning to harness the power of natural gas. Pools of this efficient and clean resource were discovered at several sites by local drillers, and the prospect of not having to pay any more lighting and heating bills caught Father Baker's attention the way it would any home-owning Buffalonian. After persuading the bishop of Buffalo to give him two thousand dollars in seed money, the priest invited a group of Pennsylvania drillers to Limestone Hill. At the conclusion of afternoon Mass, Father Baker led a procession of parishioners down his usual "prayer path," took out a small statue of Our Lady of Victory, reached down, and buried it in the ground. He instructed the drillers to begin work in that very spot.

After many weeks without success, the project was dubbed "Father Baker's Folly" by local newspapers. The foreman went to the priest and pleaded with him to give up the search. Most natural gas wells were found at a depth of six hundred feet, and the Limestone Hill drillers had already passed the thousand-foot mark. Father Baker told the man to have faith.

Finally, at the unheard-of depth of 1,137 feet, gas was struck on August 22, 1891. Victoria Well, as Father Baker named it, spouted flames into the air for many hours, causing a most miraculous scene. To this day, more than a hundred years later, Victoria Well continues to provide natural gas to some of the buildings that make up the Our Lady of Victory institutions—an incredible feat considering that most natural gas wells dry up after about thirty years.

In 1897, the protectory was expanded to 190 rooms, and the brand-new Working Boys Home was opened for eighty boys, age fifteen and up, who'd left the protectory and now had jobs in the Buffalo area. Father Baker was named vicar general of the Diocese of Buffalo in 1903 and served as the bishop's right-hand man.

Around the same time, the practice of dumping unwanted babies into the Erie Canal was becoming all too common. In response, Father Baker announced plans to construct an infant home to offer refuge, prenatal care, and adoptive services for babies and unwed mothers. The ambitious project was completed in March of 1908 and immediately filled to capacity. The Infant Home was left unlocked at night, with an empty crib standing just inside the front door. Many desperate young mothers placed their babies in that crib, and to date more than fifty thousand orphans have passed through those doors. In 1919, a maternity hospital was added.

By 1921, Father Baker was seventy-nine, his City of Charity was caring for hundreds of infants, youths, and adults each day, and he'd improved the lives of thousands of people throughout the region. However, he had one more dream that he wanted to make a reality—Our Lady of Victory Basilica. Once again, donations flooded in from around the country. European artists and architects were hired and instructed to use the finest materials available from around the world. The basilica was dedicated in May of 1926, the year of Father Baker's golden jubilee, and has since been recognized as one of the most beautiful cathedrals in the world. Our Lady of Victory is guarded by four eighteen-foot angels, and the bronze doors are an exact replica of the Grotto of Lourdes. Inside are two hundred French stained-glass windows, African mahogany pews, life-size marble statues of each of the apostles, and a 1,600-pound statue of Our Lady of Victory.

As the nation sank into the Great Depression, Father Baker's institutions served more than one million meals a year, clothed 500,000, and gave medical care to 250,000 others. On July 29, 1936, the Priest of the Poor succumbed to old age at ninety-four, in the hospital he had built. It was estimated that anywhere from 300,000 to 500,000 people viewed Father Baker's body, and the service was officiated by 700 priests. He was buried in Holy Cross Cemetery, next to the cathedral. The complex of services that Father Baker built still serves the community and is the largest employer in Lackawanna today.

Since 1986, the Our Lady of Victory parish and the Diocese of Buffalo have been working to secure canonization. Father Baker is currently Venerable, which is the first step on the path to sainthood in the Roman Catholic Church, Pope John Paul II having named him a Servant of God in 1987. Now the Vatican must review Baker's report card, accept one of his alleged miracles as the real deal, and declare him Blessed, a step called beatification. The final hurdle is a second miracle, one worked through intercession *after* beatification has been declared.

In the Sainthood Olympics, Father Baker is competing against Archbishop Fulton J. Sheen, Father Michael J. McGivney, and Father Isaac Hecker to become the first American-born male saint. And I hear that the German judge is a particularly tough grader.

To make it easier for the faithful to pray to Father Baker, he was moved inside the basilica and put under the front altar in 1999. However, the cemetery workers who dug up his coffin were surprised to find *two* coffins in his plot. Inside the smaller one were three mysterious vials of liquid. (It turns out that if you think you have a shot at sainthood, you should keep some bodily fluids on the side.) Laboratory analysis determined they contained Father Baker's blood— blood in liquid form after six decades of Buffalo winters. Saints alive! This must surely give Father Baker an edge in the quest for canonization.

Baker has been honored as Buffalo's most influential citizen of the twentieth century, and his name was given to a major bridge on New York State's Route 5. It was the late 1950s, and, in retrospect, the circumstances surrounding its construction can be seen as portentous regarding the future of the area. The memorial bridge wasn't contracted to an American firm, even though it was being built right in the backyard of Bethlehem Steel, one of the nation's largest steel producers. Instead, the girders were made in Japan and then transported across the Pacific, through the Panama Canal, up the East Coast to the Saint Lawrence Seaway, on to Lake Ontario, through the Welland Canal, and into Lake Erie. Even with all the transportation, a Japanese company was still able to provide the steel less expensively than nearby Bethlehem Steel. (Not necessarily the fault of Bethlehem Steel, since they were required by law and unions to provide workers with certain wages and benefits. And whereas Bethlehem Steel was by then considered old, Japan's plants were new, having just been built with post–World War II foreign aid, provided mostly by the United States.)

As for the bridge, it was potholed, poorly maintained, and treacherous during lake-effect storms. It eventually closed in 1991, barely thirty years old.

Another prominent Buffalo Catholic, Washington news commentator Tim Russert, mentioned Father Baker in his best-selling autobiography, *Big Russ and Me*. He fondly recalled the standard threat for South Buffalo Catholic boys caught misbehaving: "You'd better watch it or you're going to Father Baker's." When Russert unexpectedly died of a heart attack at age fifty-eight on June 13, 2008, Buffalo mayor Byron Brown ordered flags flown at half-mast, even though Russert had never held political office. And on June 18, 2008, New York senators Hillary Clinton and Chuck Schumer, along with congressman Brian Higgins, introduced a resolution to rename a section of Buffalo's US Route 20A that runs past the Buffalo Bills' home, Ralph Wilson Stadium, the "Timothy J. Russert Highway." President Bush signed the bill into law just five weeks later. Russert is buried at Rock Creek Cemetery, in Washington, DC.

Form Follows Freedom

A documentary on Western New York eccentrics would no doubt reserve a starring role for Elbert Hubbard, founder of the Roycroft movement in bucolic and picturesque East Aurora, New York, twenty miles southeast of Buffalo. Nor would it be very entertaining without this figure, who, in his day, stood at the top of the inspirational ladder the way that Dale Carnegie, Dr. Norman Vincent Peale, Anthony Robbins, and Oprah Winfrey would in years to come.

Born in 1856 in Bloomington, Illinois, Hubbard was brought to Buffalo in 1880 to sell soap products for J. D. Larkin and Company. He eventually became dissatisfied and, in 1892, at age thirty-six, left for a brief stint at Harvard. He also left his first wife and three small children for long periods of time to be with the suffragist Alice Moore, who was a freethinker like Hubbard. Additionally, Hubbard believed in free love, and in 1884, he had a daughter with Alice, and then two years later, another daughter with his wife, Bertha.

During a two-month trip to England, he was exposed to the British Arts and Crafts movement, which emphasized attractive and user-friendly products designed and made by hand, not by soulless machines on dreary factory floors. However, where the Brits were also concerned with reform and social justice, Hubbard was more taken by craftsmanship and capitalism. He arrived back in the States with a desire to start a (profitable) magazine that reflected his thoughts on morals, politics, and religion. So Hubbard returned to East Aurora in 1895 and founded the Roycroft Press, which soon expanded to furniture making, metalsmithing, leatherwork, and bookbinding. Roycroft was the surname of two seventeenth-century English printers, and though Hubbard offered different stories at different times, that's most likely where the name originated.

Based on the medieval guild system, the general idea was that making quality goods by hand would counter the dehumanizing and ill effects of the Industrial Revolution. The work and philosophy of the group had a strong influence on the development of American architecture and design in the early twentieth century. Hubbard's 1899 inspirational essay "A Message to Garcia" (Calixto García e Iñiguez was a Cuban insurgent fighting against Spanish control) ranked only behind the Bible and the dictionary in overall sales at the time. Great thinkers and artists of the day made pilgrimages to the Roycroft Campus, including Frank Lloyd Wright, Clarence Darrow, Thomas Edison, John Muir, Rudyard Kipling, Henry Steinway, Booker T. Washington, and Mark Twain.

Hubbard, often dubbed "the original hippie," became fond of eccentric dress, including a wide-brimmed Stetson hat, leather vest with gold nugget buttons, buckskin trousers, high-top boots, jangling spurs, an ascot in the plain bright red preferred by anarchists, adorned by a diamond stickpin, and a cape overcoat. He grew his hair long and sported a beard down to his waist. All this from a man who preached discipline and self-control. In 1903, Hubbard's wife divorced him, and the following year he married Alice.

At its peak in 1910, the Roycroft community had five hundred workers and served as a meeting place for radicals and reformers. Hubbard was a supporter of the Universalists, who would later merge with the Unitarians, and he worked with their local East Aurora minister, the Reverend John Sayles, on village political reform and various intellectual endeavors. "Religions are many and diverse, but reason and goodness are one," wrote Hubbard. As an example of the dichotomy of the Hubbard mind, he also said, "Formal religion was organized for slaves: it offered them consolation which earth did not provide."

When the *Titanic* sank in 1912, Hubbard wrote about the disaster and featured the story of Ida Straus, a passenger who refused to get into a lifeboat, saying, "Not I—I will not leave my husband. All these years we've traveled together, and shall we part now? No, our fate is one." Hubbard then editorialized: "Mr. and Mrs. Straus, I envy you that legacy of love and loyalty left to your children and grandchildren. The calm courage that was yours all your long and useful career was your possession in death. You knew how to do three great things—you knew how to live, how to love and how to die."

Three years later, Hubbard and his wife boarded the ocean liner *Lusitania* in New York City, bound for Liverpool. World War I was raging in Europe and the Third Reich had warned US citizens to stay out of German waters, but Hubbard insisted that he needed to interview Kaiser Wilhelm II and try to end the war. On May 7, 1915, the *Lusitania* was torpedoed and sunk by a German submarine off the coast of Ireland. The ship sank quickly, and 1,198 people died, including 128 Americans, among them Elbert and Alice Hubbard. The Germans asserted that the ship was carrying arms for the Allies (which later proved to be true). As a result, anti-German sentiment increased in the United States and rallied support to end American isolationism by sending troops abroad.

In a letter to Hubbard's son, Ernest C. Cowper, a survivor of the *Lusitania* tragedy, wrote:

> I can not say specifically where your father and Mrs. Hubbard were when the torpedoes hit, but I can tell you just what happened after that. They emerged from

their room, which was on the port side of the vessel, and came on to the boat-deck. Neither appeared perturbed in the least. Your father and Mrs. Hubbard linked arms—the fashion in which they always walked the deck—and stood apparently wondering what to do. I passed him with a baby which I was taking to a lifeboat when he said, "Well, Jack, they have got us. They are a damn sight worse than I ever thought they were." They did not move very far away from where they originally stood. As I moved to the other side of the ship, in preparation for a jump when the right moment came, I called to him, "What are you going to do?" and he just shook his head, while Mrs. Hubbard smiled and said, "There does not seem to be anything to do." The expression seemed to produce action on the part of your father, for then he did one of the most dramatic things I ever saw done. He simply turned with Mrs. Hubbard and entered a room on the top deck, the door of which was open, and closed it behind him. It was apparent that his idea was that they should die together, and not risk being parted on going into the water.

The Roycroft Shops, run by Hubbard's son, Elbert Hubbard II, operated until 1938, when they were officially declared bankrupt. However, the Roycroft Campus was granted national landmark status in 1986, taken over by a group of business leaders in 1988, and reorganized as a not-for-profit organization. Though in need of further restoration, it's open to the public and remains devoted to fostering, encouraging, and supporting artisans. There are classes, tours, and plenty of handicrafts for sale. Some of the shops play the kind of New Age music that sounds very soothing when you first hear it, and then after about ten minutes you understand why people end up with body parts in their freezer.

The Roycroft Inn, built in 1905 to accommodate all the visitors, was also under the management of Hubbard's son until 1938. After passing through several owners, it was completely restored with original and reproduction furniture and reopened in June of 1995. Carved into the doors of the rooms are the names of such notable guests as Ralph Waldo Emerson, Clara Barton, George Washington Carver, Charlotte Brontë, Henry David Thoreau, Stephen Crane, and Susan B. Anthony. And if you don't need a place to stay, the splendid restaurant is well worth a visit.

The nearby Elbert Hubbard Museum is a two-story Arts and Crafts–style bungalow built in 1910 according to a design by William Roth, the head Roycroft carpenter. It features furniture and decorative items produced by the community, along with an extensive collection of Roycroft books.

The spirit of Elbert Hubbard's iconoclasm and individualism survives in East Aurora, not just amidst its eclectic Main Street, carefully preserved homes, and old-fashioned theater, but in the hearts and minds of its residents. The village was one of the first communities to successfully block a Walmart store, in 1995 and again in 1999.

Cleveland Hill Fire

There's a reason the architecture of my school, like that of so many in the Buffalo area, is reminiscent of a maximum-security prison, and it's not because bricks, barbed wire, and asbestos happened to be on sale the year it was built. On March 31, 1954, there was a fire that would modify school design across the country, not unlike the Angola Horror had forever changed railway safety and engineering.

My friend Pete was in Mrs. Marie Morgan's third-grade class at Cleveland Hill Elementary School in Cheektowaga, New York, a suburb six miles east of the city of Buffalo. It also happened to be the school district where Pete's father, Last Chance Heffley, was superintendant. (In high school, this provided Pete with the opportunity to warn his teachers that their contracts were in his father's bureau drawer and hopefully he wouldn't accidentally throw one away.) Walter's older sister, Mary Lies, taught second grade at Cleveland Hill Elementary, and two of her children, Pete's cousins Elizabeth and Brian, were also students there. Pete recalls walking to school on an ordinary drizzly and cold late winter day and seeing his aunt Mary, who was always meticulously turned out, dressed in a light gray banker's suit.

Around lunchtime there was an explosion from the furnace in the basement boiler room and a fire broke out. Pete saw pitch black smoke billowing from the end of a hallway and was ordered, "Run!" Standing outside, he watched as teachers and then firemen ran into the blazing building to rescue children. Aunt Mary's light gray suit was soon bloodred. She'd been carrying students to safety knowing all the while that her own daughter was trapped inside, probably dead.

Walter, also a volunteer at the Cleveland Hill Fire Department, eventually had to be physically stopped from going back in to try and save people as the fire raged out of control and rescue efforts finally had to be halted. The wooden annex where music lessons were given burned to the ground. Teachers and even several students performed heroic rescues by breaking windows, some being burned in the process. Mary Lies's husband, Bert, ordered medical supplies to be sent from the nearby family drugstore, alerted hospitals, and ordered ambulances before hurrying to the scene. Meantime, passersby loaded their cars with burned children and rushed them to the hospital.

There were many local heroes that day, but nothing could compensate for the ten elementary school students who were dead, including Pete's eleven-year-old cousin, Elizabeth Lies. Five more students died of their injuries over the next few days. At least nineteen others were critically burned and would be scarred for life. When I was growing up in the 1970s, I remember meeting people my mom's age at church and at her work picnics who were badly scarred from burns, and it was always because they'd been in the Cleveland Hill fire.

Walter Heffley returned to work after the fire, but Pete believes his father had a nervous breakdown of sorts, traumatized by the ordeal and resultant loss of life. Walter had grabbed one boy from the fire by his hair, and the scalp had come off in his hand—the boy was already dead. That and other images continued to cloud his father's thoughts. Pete said his dad was never the same after the fire. Forever weighing upon Walter's mind was the fact that there'd been fifteen children in his care on that fateful day to whom he hadn't been able to give a last chance.

Following the Cleveland Hill fire, school design changed substantially across the country, as did building codes and fire prevention measures. Drilling students and faculty in emergency evacuation also increased. As a result, there've been few fatal fires in US schools since then.

Bada Bing Boom,
Black Cadillac

Buffalo and Niagara Falls were ideal locations for The Godfather movie trilogy or *The Sopranos* TV series, but the producers probably didn't want to deal with the unions. The famous expression "swim with the fishes" is said to have originated with area gangsters, since numerous waterfalls and rapids made for great dumping grounds.

Western New York has been an organized crime stronghold since the 1919 Volstead Act prohibited drinking and generously handed over to the Mafia an industry that would not only make it large sums of money, but provide entrée into other businesses that fueled the growth of crime families for the next half century. Prohibition made the Mob. And the recipients of this government largesse would go on to prove there was only one unbendable law—in cold weather, pedestrian traffic entering a building always has the right of way.

During Prohibition (1920–1933), the Mafia quickly secured a hold on the capacity to produce bathtub gin, operate speakeasies, and control the transport of liquor throughout the country. With its close proximity to Canada, where laws allowed the legal production of booze, Buffalo became a hub for bootlegging, with over a thousand cases of hooch per day crossing the border. The game was known as Cops and Wops—Irish law officers (many on the take themselves) against Italian gangsters. Mafia members riddled with bullets were known for telling police inspectors, "Nobody shot me."

From rum-running the local Mafia quickly expanded into construction, gambling, bookmaking, bribery, extortion, loan-sharking, labor and union racketeering, trucking, and narcotics trafficking. They did well, even after Prohibition ended, and so did their money laundries—businesses such as restaurants, bars, construction, real estate, waste disposal, linen supply, extermination (the other kind), and funeral parlors.

The main Buffalo-area crime family, the Magaddinos, or "The Arm," was a dominant underworld power in North America from the 1920s well into the 1980s and took the place of the old Canal Street/Dante Place's Italian "Black Hand." There was a Polish Mafia led by John "Big Korney" Kwiatowski (referenced in the 2007 hit-man comedy *You Kill Me*, starring Ben Kingsley as lead assassin Frank Falenczyk), but they were never able to pull together the sharp suits, flashy ties, two-tone shoes, and cool catchphrases, and thus had to fall back on becoming engineers, politicians, and conductors of polka bands.

The powerful boss of the local Cosa Nostra, Stefano Magaddino, was known to his family and colleagues as "Don Stefano," to locals as "The Grand Old Man," and to the media as "The Undertaker." The funeral home that served as his base of operations was said to have more than one casket go out containing two bodies, possibly accounting for some of the 150 murders for which the government believed Magaddino responsible. The funeral business turned out to be a terrific choice, considering how much business was self-generated. Meantime, the area went from being the Honeymoon Capital to the Chalk Outline Capital. By the time the 1950s rolled around, the Holy Trinity had been supplanted by Sinatra, spaghetti, and cement.

When I was eight years old, Buffalo had its first modern-day gangland-style hit, in full view of the public glare. Anyone who said there wasn't really a Mafia or that they were a thing of the past stood corrected. On May 8, 1974, Mob lieutenant John Cammilleri, who favored sharply tailored suits, pointy-toed shoes, and a pinky ring, went to a friend's wake and then to celebrate his sixty-third birthday at Romanello's

Roseland, a popular West Side Italian restaurant on Rhode Island Street. This was a place where my family regularly celebrated birthdays after my mom closed our kitchen and returned to school to earn a nursing degree. We loved the way they made Caesar salads and flaming desserts right at the table, a budding pyromaniac's dream come true. Only, we didn't happen to be there that fateful spring night, or else I would've had a really good story for show-and-tell the next day.

However, we'd been there the week before. I clearly remember the occasion because my mother and I went to the restroom together and she said, "Why is your skirt on that dirty floor?" (You could sandblast and then shine a floor until it glowed and it would always be a cesspool to her. A relative recently confessed that she runs through her house with air freshener right before my mother arrives.)

By the age of eight, I'd already discovered how dense my mother could be. "Because I'm going to the bathroom," I informed her.

"You pull a skirt up, not take it down!" she announced through the stall door. That's why I never wore skirts in the first place—because they were so incredibly stupid. And it wasn't as if they came with an instruction book. Like many girls my age who were making the transition to a pants-only life, I'd been permanently scarred as a three-year-old by supershort dresses caught atop frilly white underpants, tights where the crotch remained around knee level, and saddle shoes with slippery, smooth leather soles. It was a recipe not only for disaster but for a toddler peep show.

On the night of May 8, as John Cammilleri walked from his car to the restaurant door, someone called his name. He turned to look, shots rang out, and he was hit in the chest and face. Cammilleri fell to the ground, dead. Customers inside the restaurant came running out to see a car with four men in it speeding down Chenango Street. Writing about the event years later, *Buffalo News* reporter Michael Beebe employed the bad old days' tabloid-style heading "Wake Proved Deadly." Intrepid BuffaloRising.com went with the brightly alliterative "No Calamari for Cammilleri," in their commemorative piece.

Leo J. Donovan, then commander of the Buffalo Homicide Squad, described the shooting in classic gangland terms. "It smacks pretty much of a planned job, with a finger man to point him out, a trigger man who could shoot accurately in poor lighting, a wheelman who knew the streets, and possibly a background man to keep an eye on the finger man."

Despite rumors that police and federal officials knew who the perpetrators were, the crime remains unsolved to this day. However, FBI reports indicate that Cammilleri's murder ignited a wave of fifteen Mob-related hits that lasted through the 1980s, with only one case ending in an arrest.

The Racketeer Influenced and Corrupt Organizations Act (RICO) was passed in 1970, thereby giving law enforcement greater freedom to pursue criminal acts performed as part of an ongoing crime organization. *Omertà*, the code of silence, became less popular since a single drug bust could now result in a life sentence. And the US Federal Witness Protection Program made it possible for Mob members to cut deals and stay out of prison in exchange for testimony.

Legendary Mafia boss of bosses Stefano Magaddino died of a heart attack on June 19, 1974, at the age of eighty-two, after a fifty-two-year reign as area crime family capo. He had a proper Catholic funeral and was buried at Saint Joseph's Cemetery in Niagara Falls, New York.

Everyone agrees that, much like the Buffalo winters, the Buffalo Mafia is not what it once was. Lawyers who used to defend crime family members will tell you how the Mob's secondary businesses, originally set up as fronts and money laundries, became so successful that they're now legitimate full-time operations. Try the capicola sub at La Nova pizzeria, where the motto is "Our Customers Are Our Family," and see for yourself.

Unfortunately, that hasn't left the area free from vice. In November of 2008, former Niagara Falls mayor Vince Anello pleaded not guilty to four felony charges stemming from an FBI investigation into allegations of political corruption. *The Sopranos* and Niagara Falls appear to have both gone into reruns.

A Tale of Two Eddies

Growing up in the 1970s BC (Before Cablevision), we had three network channels to choose from, plus the sci-fi sounding UHF, so for many hours of the day there was nothing good on unless you happened to be a fan of bowling, soap operas, or *The 700 Club*. It was hardly worth the hike from the pleather couch to the low-definition TV set to change channels. And after midnight, most stations "went off the air," leaving behind a color-bar test pattern or else black and white flecks called "snow." Thankfully, infomercials have since rescued us from such cruel sensory deprivation.

I was four years old when *Sesame Street* mercifully arrived on the screen. Though a cutting-edge teaching tool, the early shows are notable for their depiction of women as strictly secondary characters, basically as they were to be found in real life back then. Males reigned supreme on The Street—Bert and Ernie, Oscar the Grouch, Mr. Snuffleupagus, Elmo, Count Von Count, Big Bird, and Grover. A woman couldn't even be trusted with the difference between *near* and *far*, which demonstrates how far they were from equality. On the fun side, the show was also a lot less psychologically correct back then—Oscar was totally grouchy, Big Bird had an invisible friend, and Cookie Monster frantically stuffed himself with nonorganic, high-fat cookies.

My favorite cartoon show, *Popeye*, turns out to have been its own hospital of eating disorders. Popeye ate only spinach. Wimpy ate only hamburgers. Bluto ate everything. And poor skinny Olive Oyl ate nothing or else had one horrendous case of bulimia.

If that wasn't excitement enough, local television shows occasionally featured Marge Facklam from the Buffalo Zoo talking about an animal that I secretly hoped would go berserk. Facklam was the head of education at the zoo and would also make the rounds to area schools and day camps. Luckily for us, she was very partial to reptiles, as were we, and this was probably the reason why she was constantly being called to get snakes off chandeliers and out from behind stoves.

The Buffalo Zoo sits on 23.5 acres in Delaware Park, and in addition to the standard mammals, snakes, and birds, it features a pinktoe tarantula and a red-headed centipede. The zoo was started when a successful furrier named Jacob E. Bergtold donated a pair of deer to the City of Buffalo. Were deer scarce back then? On my way to high school in the early 1980s, it was hard not to hit a deer. To provide the deer room to graze and keep them from ruining everyones' gardens, Elam R. Jewett, the publisher of *The Buffalo Daily Journal*, offered to let the deer roam on his estate, which many other deer were probably doing already, but on the down low.

It happened that plans were in the works for a park that would give residents a place to stroll and socialize, so renowned landscape architect Frederick Law Olmsted incorporated the zoo into his design for what is now Delaware Park. More animals were soon donated. A couple of beavers people found in their backyards? A brace of squirrels? The first building was opened in 1875, making the Buffalo Zoological Gardens the nation's third oldest zoo.

During the Great Depression, the zoo actually expanded as it became a major site for Franklin Delano Roosevelt's Works Progress Administration, part of the New Deal legislation to get America back in the black and prove that the country was too big to fail. Marlin Perkins was hired as curator in 1938 and developed the animal collection to be what was considered one of the finest in the country, all the while demonstrating once again how animals are superior to children—it's perfectly acceptable to buy and sell their offspring. Under his guidance, the Reptile House opened in 1942 with more than four hundred specimens. People my age know Marlin Perkins as host of the popular television series *Wild Kingdom*, where his trusty assistant Jim would go upstream and wrestle the grizzly bear while he stayed back and kept a close eye out for ripples in the goldfish pond. The show was sponsored by Mutual of Omaha, which resulted in not-so-subtle product placements such as, "Just as that mother black bear protects her cubs from a harsh and unpredictable world, you can protect your family with life insurance!"

There was a famous chimp at the zoo named Eddie who'd been a star to Buffalo schoolchildren in the 1940s and '50s. In fact, there's now a statue of him at the Buffalo Museum of Science, though it's usually kept in storage. By the time I met Eddie in the late sixties, he may as well have been auditioning for a reality TV show called *When Good Chimps Go Bad*. Visitors had become moving targets for spitting, peeing, and the daily hurling of the fruit salad.

Jeremiah Horrigan, who worked at the zoo in the early seventies, reminisced about Eddie in a 2007 *Times Herald-Record* column. "Everybody loved Eddie. But the burden of amusing humans and living in a cell had taken its toll long before I arrived there. By then, Eddie was a moody, glowering wreck. Parents used to stand outside his cell and tell their kids how Eddie was a star back in their day. The kids would take one look at the hostile, hollow-eyed Eddie squatting in the corner of his cell, then look back at their parents in utter mystification."

Eddie serves as a good example of why zoos began to change into places that were more animal-centric and not just display cases for humans to enjoy peering into. In 2002, the Buffalo Zoo began a fifteen-year, $75 million renovation that's providing more-naturalistic habitats and enhancing exhibits. M&T Bank has sponsored the wonderful Rainforest Falls, which leads me to wonder where corporate adoption was when I was growing up during the 1970s recession. We'd have happily signed on to be the Tops Markets Pedersen Family exhibit for a monthly stipend, or perhaps just some fresh fruit and hearty grains while inflation was going gangbusters.

Meantime, there was another famous Eddie working the downtown Buffalo area back in the seventies and eighties. This was a guy with no legs who scooted around on a wheelie board, usually in the vicinity of Main and Huron streets. He carried a tin cup in one hand and a transistor radio in the other, to which he bopped while directing comments to women passersby. More often than not, his remarks were lewd, and sometimes Eddie lifted their skirts (which happened to be at his eye level), and this would result in the police arresting him.

However, when the cops tried to bring Eddie from the jail cell to the courtroom for his arraignment, he'd bite them. So they'd get a leftover refrigerator box, dump him in that, and drag it into the courtroom. The judge would be horrified and take the cops aside to ask what they thought they were doing. The cops all replied with the same line: "I'm not touching him. You get him out if you want him." A few hours later, Eddie was back out on Main Street, bopping to his radio and whistling at women.

School Days—
A Few Flakes Short
of a Snowball

For kids, autumn in Western New York revolved around foliage and Halloween back when I was growing up. Many joyous hours were spent raking rivers of orange, gold, yellow, and scarlet leaves into an enormous pile, playing in them, reraking them, leaping into them (and this time leaving the mess for Dad), and then taking the biggest and most brilliant ones and carefully ironing them between sheets of wax paper. These in turn would become bookmarks, place mats, and collages. Parents took us on car rides to gaze at the many trees changing color like living fireworks and kept telling us to "Look, look how beautiful it is, stop hitting her, you're not looking!" And so now we hate hearing how beautiful the leaves are, and we don't care if we ever see another one.

Because of rampant inflation, candy prices tripled during my peak sugar years, so my friends and I not only loved Halloween but we needed it to stockpile the treats that would keep us alive until Christmas. Local factories kept laying people off, while a lower tax base meant cuts in civil service jobs, along with hospital and sanitation positions. Parents struggled to pay for heat for the house and gas for the car, so when it came to such childhood necessities as Gobstoppers, Razzles, Chuckles, Bottle Caps, and Bubble Yum, they were tighter than the faux forest mural glued to our dining room wall. Thus we spent months planning our costumes and trick-or-treat route for maximum return on investment. Back then, girls did not dress as streetwalkers because (1) high heels would slow you down; (2) our parents wouldn't have allowed it (Catholic mothers knew that whatever clothes you died in were what you'd wear throughout eternity); and, most importantly, (3) it was already too cold by then. No one had heard of global warming, and from where we were standing, wearing parkas and overshoes in October, global freezing appeared to be of much greater concern.

For me, Halloween was merely a coin toss. My natural fright wig of unruly strawberry blond hair left only the Cowardly Lion from *The Wizard of Oz* or Cousin Itt from *The Addams Family* as costume possibilities. Still, I was able to tell people that I was a model, since my mother's good friend wrote nursing textbooks and used us for the accompanying photographs. I'm the one wearing the cervical collar.

In my local public school, kids were separated by ability. They gave our first-grade reading groups cutesy inspirational names such as Cheetahs, Jaguars, and Blue Jays. Still unable to form words using letters, I was classified as a Dinosaur. I tried not to read too much into it, but since I couldn't read at all, that really wasn't possible, aside from a vague feeling that I'd been marked for extinction. It was not unlike the day my teacher dropped the bomb that *y* could sometimes be used as a vowel, and I was so discombobulated that I couldn't remember more than one verse to "Kumbaya" during the sing-along after lunch. And that was saying a lot since the neighborhood was 80 percent Catholic and everyone knew at least eighteen verses, while a really good elementary school teacher could do the deaf version too.

But Fortuna spun her mighty wheel and the fickle finger of placement fate rewrote destiny when my seventh-grade homeroom teacher slumbered through the Otis-Lennon School Ability Test and we treated it as a group project. Didn't they wonder why everyone with a last name starting with Ob to Pr had IQs of 150 while the rest of the school averaged 103? A couple kids previously heading for careers at Midas Muffler were now on the fast track, and suddenly Mensa was calling.

The area in which we all seemed to fall down, teachers and students alike, was the metric system. We were supposed to discard our demented method of measurement that involved the length of some old king's foot, Egyptian forearms, and double-stepping Romans, and replace it with a system divisible by ten, as the reasonable Canadians had done years earlier. Yet, to this day, Americans in hospitals and doctor's offices across the country have the magnitude of their various lumps explained not in sensible scientific terms, but in the language of fruits, nuts, and vegetables. Rather than be informed that some mass has a perimeter of two or twenty centimeters, we're told the nodule is the size of a garbanzo bean, the tumor is on par with an acorn squash, or the growth is larger than a macadamia nut but smaller than an apricot. American universities should offer a double major of oncology and horticulture.

In a similar fashion, grammar went out the schoolhouse window, evidenced by the fact that a best-selling children's album of the era had the pronoun-challenged title *Free To Be...You and Me*. Other recording artists were having *lay* versus *lie* issues, as was the case with Bob Dylan's "Lay, Lady, Lay" and Eric Clapton's "Lay Down Sally," unless these were supposed to be clever double entendres or else not-so-sly references similar to the drug-encrypted "Lucy in the Sky with Diamonds." Subject-verb agreement was next in the syntax firing line with The Police singing, "Everything she do just turn me on."

But make no mistake about it, school was important! There was no safety net, trust fund, or backup plan in my recession-scarred neighborhood. It was before grade inflation, student self-esteem, and protein shakes. If you decided not to study one night and did poorly on just a single test, it could ruin your average and your chances of getting into a good college, and you'd end up as *riffraff*, living in a decrepit bungalow on the wrong side of the tracks with mean dogs and a rusty jalopy in the front yard, on the slippery slope to becoming the town drunk with the village idiot as your only friend and a twenty-five-year GED reunion the solitary invitation on your refrigerator.

At least this was true if you weren't a candidate for a sports scholarship, and I was no more likely to win one than I was likely to win a beauty pageant. Still, I enjoyed a four-year career on the soccer team, one distinguished more by attendance than prowess and largely a result of the fact that our Born Again Christian coach's philosophy was more "equal opportunity" than "go for the gold." He praised "good energy." Also, he told me the *real* locations of the games, which is more than I can say for the neighborhood kickball hooligans.

Title IX, the 1972 law that prohibited discrimination in federally financed activities, thereby declaring equal funding and facilities for girls' sports, hadn't quite taken hold yet. We were just crawling out of the primordial Crisco ooze of the home economics (or domestic sciences) wing, and girls' sports had only a 7 percent participation rate in 1972, compared to the 50 percent it has today. As a result, my girls' varsity soccer team was issued the discarded uniforms of the boys' junior varsity soccer team. The fabric was somewhere between tent canvas and Silly Putty, which, despite causing a few strange rashes, didn't shrink or wrinkle or even really bend, for that matter. And without darts or extra room for the female figure, the jerseys acted as an early version of the as-yet-to-be-invented sports bra. This fabulous prison-farm look was finished off with long white tube socks that when pulled all the way up resembled go-go boots. Before it was warm enough to practice outside (basically anywhere above freezing), we had to take a bus from our high school to an elementary school and back every day after school because the coaches didn't want us scuffing up the floor of the boys' gym. So whenever you see a woman over forty supporting a female presidential candidate, it's not that the voter agrees with all of the nominee's policies so much as that she played sports at a public school prior to 1980 with wads of polyester chafing her thighs and armpits.

School is expensive nowadays, and kids require all sorts of stuff, like iPods, laptops, cell phones, and prescription drugs. Instead of book bags, they need not just backpacks, but backpacks on wheels—actual luggage that makes it look as if they're going to catch the shuttle to the airport for a week of meetings in Chicago. When I was growing up, we had windup toys, Etch A Sketch, and glow-in-the-dark yo-yos, but nothing with a fun factor that was deemed worthy to drag to class. The school banned slingshots and squirt guns. And there was not yet a need for an official policy statement on automatic weapons and Tasers. You were as likely to bring your father's shotgun to middle school as you were a can of your mother's Tab. Not happening.

Back then, if we were jonesing for something it was usually a Snickers bar or a Slurpee, so we went to the kitchen where everything reusable was kept—basically paper plates, tea bags, and butcher string—wet a piece of bloody butcher string, tied it around the loosest tooth in our mouth, and attached it to the garage door. Voilà. Next day the tooth fairy came and we had a dollar. What could be easier?

Suffering the humiliation of Amherst's unfortunately named Sweet Home School District was sadly made worse by a home improvement store called The Busy Beaver located right next to the middle school back in my day. And with the recent addition of a million-dollar auditorium, the school now resembles a prison for the performing arts. However, after years of insisting that the school system's architecture was Soviet-inspired functionalism at its worst and clearly suggested that the Geneva Conventions could be discarded while authority looked the other way, I silenced the scorn after a recent visit to the Amherst Museum. On display was the original one-room Sweet Home schoolhouse, built in 1847 for $125, which had an *outhouse*. Now I absolutely adore those turd brown bricks of yore. Why not bring back the turquoise trim?

In fact, I'd love to be a student at my old high school today because now you can wear shorts and sweatpants. Actually, we didn't think we had it so bad in jeans and sneakers, since our mothers had to wear skirts and saddle shoes. Meantime, girlfriends who attended Catholic school slyly hemmed up their skirts a few inches until one day the nuns would haul them all into the cafeteria, measure the skirts with a yardstick, rip out the hems of the skirts that were too short, and send the girls home to their Singer push-pedal sewing machines. This doesn't happen nowadays for a number of reasons, largely because most high school girls no longer even own a needle and thread.

Traversing the old school corridors, I am most pleased to see that in health class they still use skinny, pasty-faced Resuscitation Annie, in the blue tracksuit, to teach CPR. And she still looks like she died from a heroin overdose. "Annie, Annie! Are you okay?"

How I Was Exposed

Following high school graduation, I spent a number of years on Wall Street valuing things, mostly stocks and bonds, determining what a share of X is worth right now. Well, *now* obviously next to nothing. However back then, we had formulas to make such calculations for everything from index options to soybean futures.

But how do you value art? What *is* the value of art—what someone will pay for it? How it makes us feel? And how do you put a price on that?

Growing up in the Buffalo area during the seventies, my family didn't have much disposable income, like most people at the time, because it all went to the Niagara Mohawk power company, and we weren't particularly sophisticated, though we knew enough to have gold shag carpeting, a sand sculpture, spider plants in macramé hangers, and a bottle of Blue Nun on hand for company. Still, on the salaries of a nurse and a court reporter we had access to an amazing amount of culture—concerts, plays, dance, exhibitions, museums, galleries, craft fairs, poetry readings, and festivals. At the height of the Blizzard of '77, locals didn't yell and curse—they went on television singing "Send in the Plows" to the city's head of transportation.

Watching *Peter Pan* at the Studio Arena Theatre when I was seven made me think that I could fly. I couldn't, and it ended badly, but you never know until you try. Art makes you dream big. And like Picasso's *Guernica*, it can also deliver a big dose of reality along with an introduction to the concept of negative space.

I saw Andrés Segovia play classical guitar one particularly stormy night when I was eleven and suffering from one heck of a case of bronchitis. As other people live with cancer or AIDS, the children of Western New York lived with upper respiratory distress. If we'd stayed home for every case of walking pneumonia, pleurisy, or whooping cough, we'd have been shut-ins the first eighteen years of our lives.

However, I was terrified that I'd cough or sneeze during the great Segovia's performance, and so right before the curtain rose I hacked and hacked and honked and honked. The dowager to my left turned, lowered her opera glasses, and inquired, "Do you plan on doing that all throughout the performance?" I said, "No, ma'am, I am getting it all out now."

Then a small man, almost ninety years old, walked out onto that enormous stage at Shea's Buffalo Theater, a stage where we'd watched knights on horseback in *Camelot* and the goings-on of an entire Thai village in *The King and I*. One small man on a stool, who didn't speak to us in English, filled that large stage and that enormous theater for over two hours, transporting us from the cold and snow to someplace warm and romantic with the soaring melodies of his Spanish guitar. I wanted to move to Andalusia, take guitar lessons, and wear thick glasses with dark black, heavy square frames.

My mom and dad took me to shows at Shea's, Studio Arena, Artpark, Melody Fair, the Aud, UB's Katharine Cornell Theatre, and Kleinhans Music Hall, and many more wonderful productions at local churches, synagogues, and event spaces. I remember how we'd walk across Main Street and see people in Dada attire prophesying end-times in loud voices (turns out they were right), talking to themselves, and even fighting with themselves. My mom, a psychiatric nurse, would explain that they had problems and most likely thought they were talking to other people. Being an only child, I could certainly understand the value of having an imaginary friend, but I remember thinking, *Wouldn't you choose someone you got along with so it'd be fun to do things together?*

Nowadays you walk down Main Street and people are all yammering into their cell phones and *everyone* looks like they're living on cloud cuckoo if you don't see those little wires coming out of their heads. Maybe you'd call it installation art, or art of the moment. My mother the nurse would call it people not watching where they're going who will end up in the paraplegic ward at Erie County Medical Center, and don't call her when it happens because she told you so. Now that everyone has cell phones, my mom says you have to identify crazy people by looking at their shoes. Only I don't know what to look for.

My Sweet Home Junior High School English class went to see a matinee of *A Christmas Carol*, and kids sitting in the row directly in front of us threw pennies onto the stage and my class got the blame. Even worse, it was the seventies so the actors picked them up.

On another class trip, a world-renowned danseur was performing in George Balanchine's *Jewels* when he fell and improvised a somersault off the stage. I realized that no matter how famous you are and how much you practice, shit can still go wrong.

The real show that night was on the way home, when the big yellow school bus went down West Chippewa Street at eleven o'clock. It was 1978. You want to talk about art? The neighborhood was a media presentation so mixed that it included silver Spandex. That you could dress fur up or down I guess I was aware of. But fuchsia fur hot pants? No, that was definitely something new.

By age fifteen, I knew almost every work in the Albright-Knox Art Gallery. Pete was studying to become a docent, so I'd hold up flash cards with pictures of the paintings and sculptures and quiz him. I hate to admit that I did this in exchange for food at Burger King and not for art's sake, but as an adult I remember the French artists van Gogh and Gauguin and the French fries all with equal appreciation.

My artist friend Russell Ram, who won the gold medal at the National Collage Society annual exhibit and has his work in the permanent collection of the Burchfield Penney Art Center, says that Western New York has always been a supportive community for artists. This is evidenced not only by the number of artists, galleries, museums, and private collections, but the fact that the Buffalo Society of Artists, founded in 1891, is one of the oldest continuously operating arts organizations in the country. "Despite its reputation as being a blue-collar town, art has always been a large part of the fabric of the Buffalo area community."

My elementary school teachers were fond of saying, "That which does not kill you makes you stronger." Inspiration comes from all places. If you'd told me that writing about waiting for the bus with snot frozen to my face would later become my art, I wouldn't have believed it, but as usual, those teachers were right.

When we experience art, we can never know what will come of it. There's a woman who's seen *The Sound of Music* more than a thousand times. Maybe she misunderstood the line "With songs they have sung for a thousand years," or maybe that musical is the art that speaks to her.

I volunteer at the Booker T. Washington Learning Center, in East Harlem, where we struggle to find enough time to work on reading, math, and science. But what always takes precedence is exposure to art—dance performances, plays and musicals, concerts, sculpture presentations, visits to botanical gardens, architecture tours. We drop everything if we can get tickets to a show or an exhibit.

Because even when we don't know the exact value of art—whether a work sells for a dollar or a million dollars, if it's at the Allentown Art Festival or in the Albright-Knox— we intrinsically understand that it's powerful, sometimes ineffable, and, most important, transformative.

For instance, there were forty-eight professional Elvis impersonators in 1977. Now there are 116,328, and that doesn't include the flying Elvises, or would that be Elvi? Anyway, if this growth rate continues, by the year 2025 one in four people will be an Elvis impersonator.

Arborgeddon

Buffalonians love this story: It was late fall and the Indians asked their chief if the coming winter was going to be cold or mild. Since he was a chief in modern society, he'd never been taught the old ways, and when he looked at the sky he couldn't tell what the winter was going to be like. To be on the safe side, he told his tribe the winter was indeed going to be cold, and that members should collect plenty of firewood. But being a practical leader, he also called the National Weather Service and asked, "Is the coming winter supposed to be cold?" The meteorologist responded, "It looks like this winter is going to be quite cold." So the chief went back to his people and told them to collect even more firewood in order to be prepared. A week later he called the National Weather Service again. "Does it still look like it's going to be a very cold winter?" "Yes," the man at the National Weather Service again replied. "It's going to be a very cold winter." The chief went back to his people and ordered them to collect every scrap of firewood they could find. Two weeks later, the chief called the National Weather Service. "Are you absolutely sure that the winter is going to be very cold?" "Absolutely," the man replied. "It's looking more and more like it's going to be one of the worst winters we've ever seen." "How can you be so sure?" the chief asked. The weatherman replied, "The Indians are collecting firewood like crazy." And that pretty much sums up weather forecasting in Western New York.

You can't write about Buffalo without storm stories. And there have been many. In November of 1837, a mighty gale killed dozens, destroyed the waterfront, and deposited several ships onto the city's streets. A sudden shift in wind on October 18, 1844, resulted in a disastrous flood. Once again, ships were destroyed on the lake or washed ashore, and the streets of Buffalo were strewn with nautical wreckage. More than two hundred people lost their lives, many of whom were stacked for identification in front of City Hall, Terrance Market, and the courthouse. On November 7, 1913, a blizzard known as the Big Blow, with ninety-mile-an-hour winds and thirty-five-foot waves, hit the Great Lakes, leaving nineteen ships sunk, nineteen swept ashore, and more than 250 people dead, with damages exceeding $100 million in today's dollars.

In March of 1936, Saint Patrick's Day went from green to white faster than you can sing "McNamara's Band" when almost two feet of snow fell on the city over the course of a single afternoon. The celebration moved indoors, and one assumes there weren't any complaints about warm beer.

On Christmas Eve day of 1945 came the worst blizzard in Buffalo's history up until that point. Not only was the city shut down, but the trains couldn't get through, and thousands of soldiers trying to get home for the holidays were stranded.

In the movie *Chisum*, John Wayne's character famously says, "Round up everybody that can ride a horse or pull a trigger." In blizzard-prone Buffalo this might be paraphrased as "Round up everybody that can ride a plow or push a shovel." The Blizzard of '77, a.k.a. the Storm of the Century, which struck on January 28, 1977, when I was in the sixth grade, resulted in approximately twenty-five deaths from people being trapped in cars, having heart attacks while shoveling snow, and automobile accidents. It was actually a series of back-to-back blizzards, and when President Jimmy Carter, instead of going in person, sent his son Chip to assess the damage, another storm was predicted, and I'm pretty sure the president was afraid if he *did* make it to Buffalo he might not get back out again until spring.

In the middle of the Blizzard of '77, Buffalo zookeepers delivered a baby camel and had to beat back rumors that a rogue polar bear had escaped by climbing a snowdrift, although three reindeer and two sheep *had* escaped that way, with one intrepid reindeer determined to visit the suburbs, hoofing it three miles to Kenmore, probably on his way to the Herschell Carrousel Factory Museum, in North Tonawanda. And snowmobiling was banned in some areas for fear that riders would run into chimneys.

Thousands of people were stranded at home, and in addition to record ratings for the TV miniseries *Roots*, such close captivity resulted in a blizzard baby boomlet nine months later. With the number of folks stuck in hotel bars, there may have also been a few babies fathered by Glen Grant, Johnnie Walker, and Jim Beam.

The Blizzard of '77 is perhaps the first snowstorm to become fully merchandised, with a board game, a set of six glasses with reproductions of *Buffalo Courier Express* articles featuring the storm, a Blizzard Ball to commemorate the event, two full-length books, a documentary, and a song by Ontario band Alexisonfire called "Crisis." (Some listeners hearing the phrase "end of the world" in this song have drawn parallels to the crisis in the Middle East; however, I find it more of a rallying cry aimed at the future inventors of polar fleece.) In the meantime, this survivor anxiously awaits a Blizzard of '77 PEZ dispenser.

During the Blizzard of '85, our constantly quotable mayor, Jimmy Griffin, advised residents to "Go home, watch Channel 7, and get a six-pack of Genny [local beer] and stay home," thus earning him the nickname "Jimmy Six-Pack." Buffalo, with its preponderance of watering holes, has never been much of a Prohibition town. During the cholera epidemic of 1832, Mayor Dr. Ebenezer Johnson advised locals to mix brandy with their drinking water.

Novelist Frank Norris's assertion that the only "story cities" in the United States are New York, San Francisco, and New Orleans was clearly made by a man who hadn't lived through a Great Lakes squall or a Western New York blizzard. Weather will continue to come and go, but a storm is a story with a beginning, a middle, and an end. And everyone in and around Buffalo has a storm story. Most people have a few. During the Blizzard of '77, my friend Pete ended up at the home of two strangers who dropped anchor in a case of Cutty Sark and by the end of the night were insisting that they'd written the hit Broadway musical *West Side Story*.

Retired Buffalo teacher Bonnie Botsford says, "The saddest story was the printing plant on Fuhrman Boulevard. It was snowed in, and the people who worked there were stranded for days with partial copies of Harlequin Romances. If there was ever anything worse for a machinist to be stuck with than a Harlequin Romance, it might have to be a *partial* Harlequin Romance."

Maybe I'm just getting old and so when recalling my Amherst childhood I could swear times were so much tougher that we walked to school uphill both ways under an asbestos sky wearing twice our body weight in wool clothing, but it does seem that there are more snow days since we've started hearing about climate change. Back in the seventies and early eighties, I remember watching ominous pewter clouds darken the horizon in the late afternoon and by nightfall it would be snowing hard. I made the executive decision that there was no point in doing homework or studying for tests since surely school would be closed the following day. It was, instead, time for staying up late and making plans to go sledding and drink hot chocolate with friends. In my predominantly Catholic neighborhood, many weather-related prayers were said on those nights, though in most cases the hopes of the parents conflicted with those of their children.

Normally my mother slept late because she worked the zombie shift at a local nursing home, but when it had snowed a lot during the night I could hear the radio on in the kitchen—a good sign. Lots of community activities, dance classes, and bingo games were canceled. However, the alphabetical list of school closings seemed endless, in large part because the Sweet Home School District came after the word *Saint*, which in the Buffalo area entailed numerous listings. These were always followed by Starpoint High School, which seemed to shutter in the event of a light rain. I imagine thirty-year-olds still trying to put together enough gym classes for a diploma.

Then I would hear it—not the name *Sweet Home* on the radio, but the unmistakable sound of the old double-clutch bus with a top speed of thirty-five miles per hour that shot out enough exhaust to make a kindergartner light-headed (the first cousin to a fresh ditto contact high, where we shoved our faces into that intoxicating purple ink as if it were raw cookie dough). The early bus was rounding the corner of Frankhauser Road to pick up the athletic overachievers for an hour of swimming or weightlifting before classes began. School was definitely open.

Aside from the Blizzard of '77, it seemed as if Sweet Home never closed, no matter how cold and blustery it was outside. You'd have thought they were purposely trying to get rid of us to reduce class sizes. Nowadays, local area schools appear to close at the first hint of a storm. It doesn't make sense since back in my day mothers were home to take care of kids on a snow day and now so many work. One would think that with better buses and snow removal technology it'd be just the opposite. People say this is because we live in a much more litigious society, but I have another theory.

In the old days, when the drivers of busloads of schoolchildren found the roads becoming impassable, they made for the nearest firehouse and dumped off their charges. I think our local firefighters eventually decided either (1) their time was better spent dealing with actual emergencies; or (2) running into burning buildings was preferable to coping with sixty elementary school children jazzed up on apple juice and sugar cookies singing "John Jacob Jingleheimer Schmidt" over and over. And over.

By the third week of December 2001, people had almost given up on having a white Christmas when flakes finally started to fall the day beforehand. Almost two feet of snow was on the ground by Christmas Eve, and within a week over seven feet had made landfall. Aside from Christmas itself, most events were canceled, including a performance of a play called *Lake Effect,* which was set in Buffalo during the Blizzard of '77. Talk about Erie irony.

You know you're in for something special when the National Weather Service says they've "never seen anything like it before!" and the only folks heading into the area are a crew from the (Really Bad) Weather Channel. Basically, they're talking about a meteorological event that you can't even find in the Bible, which is rather well-known for its over-the-top weather conditions. The storm that hit Western New York on October 12, 2006, made for the two snowiest October days recorded in Buffalo since the National Weather Service began keeping track 137 years earlier, and it left 400,000 residents without power for days and in some cases weeks. When heavy wet snow accumulated on trees that still had most of their leaves, it snapped them in half or broke limbs, which brought down power lines as they fell.

Workers at the region's National Weather Service office were, for reasons known only to them, naming storms after insects that year, so it officially became Lake Storm Aphid. This was a tiny name for what would turn out to be an enormous tempest. Newspapers and radio announcers quickly chimed in with catchier monikers, such as the October Surprise Storm, Arborgeddon, the Columbus Day Massacre, and my favorite, the Freaky Friday the 13th Storm. Journalists, like nature, can always be counted upon to fill a vacuum.

The quirky storm dumped several feet of snow in some places and hardly an inch half a mile away, or else no snow at all. The town of Tonawanda was considered ground zero, as almost no home escaped damage. Locals, who are hardly unaccustomed to snowstorms, were baffled by the unusual behavior of this one, which was often accompanied by thunder and lightning and gusty winds—a rare meteorological phenomenon called "thundersnow"—and the crack of tree limbs breaking off, which sounded like exploding firecrackers. The end result was a twenty-square-mile region that looked as if it had been bombed.

Nearly every school in Western New York was closed, along with many businesses. Buffalo Niagara International Airport delayed or canceled almost all flights. Stores selling generators quickly ran out. The New York State gubernatorial race was halted in its tracks when Democrat Eliot Spitzer and Republican John Faso, who were in town for a debate, found the campaign trail cold and the exits blocked. One can only wonder if future governor Spitzer (a.k.a. Client #9) found a way to keep warm.

Local news offered instructions about the life span of perishables in freezers that had lost power. With the temp hovering around thirty-four degrees, it wasn't quite cold enough to employ the old Buffalo trick of converting the garage into a walk-in freezer, but putting milk and eggs in a bag outside could still achieve refrigeration. Others turned to backyard grills as a way to use up whatever meat had thawed.

On the heels of the storm, a flood watch went into effect, and also a driving ban in Buffalo, Tonawanda, and Amherst, where 80 percent of the roads were impassable. Traffic was prohibited on a 110-mile stretch of Thruway between Rochester and Dunkirk. Even the Peace Bridge border crossing, between the United States and Canada, had to be closed. Mayor Byron Brown issued an official "boil water advisory" since many of the municipal electric water pumps were no longer operational. The National Guard was called in with lifts and dump trucks to deal with an estimated 30 million tons of trees and other debris left over from the storm.

Reminiscent of the Blizzard of '77, the areas most affected by the storm were declared a major disaster area by the president, this time George W. Bush, on October 24, 2006. About 90 percent of the trees had been damaged and approximately 57,000 of them died. An enormous replanting effort, undertaken mostly by volunteers, continues to this day.

Conservative estimates to clean up after the storm were at least $130 million, but they continued to rise. Thirteen people perished during the storm as a result of car accidents, being crushed by a falling tree limb, carbon monoxide poisoning, and preexisting health conditions. Several hundred died in the aftermath, some from chainsaw accidents and more from carbon monoxide poisoning, a result of running generators inside homes.

If you're not convinced that Buffalonians are devoted to their sports teams, let the record show that despite debris-clogged roads and downed power lines, the sold-out hockey game at HSBC Arena in downtown Buffalo went on, and the undefeated Sabres beat the Rangers 7–4, with full attendance of 18,690. Thousands more listened to the game from home in the dark using battery-powered radios. Beating the Red Wings on Friday (3–2), the Rangers on Saturday (7–4), and then the Flyers two days later (9–1) was said to have helped people through the storm more than anything else.

Some years, people have been found Rollerblading in December, and the winter carnival has been canceled for a lack of, well, winter. But then it all comes roaring back, and suddenly everyone is saying global warming, global shwarming. We'll wait for the next Al Gore movie to come out on video.

In the meantime, the Western New York holiday gift list is: generator, chain saw, wood chipper, carbon monoxide detector, Yaktrax (chains for your shoes), Buffalo Sabres Snuggie. And because a diamond ring can be used to cut ice off your frozen windshield, when choosing that rock, gals should be sure to explain why it has to be big—a ten-carat ring could save your life!

Few would argue with the cold-weather principle that it's best to rake early and remove dead tree limbs in a timely manner. But other practices are more subjective. For instance, in wintertime you find out that people have very different driving philosophies, and it's best to travel with those who hold one closest to your own. The Utilitarians, aiming for the greatest good for the greatest number, turn off the radio (because obviously this impedes visibility), put on the flashers, stay in the right-hand lane, and press their faces against the windshield. The Objectivists ("I'll do what's best for me and to hell with everyone else") double up on speed in order to make it home before the storm gets any worse, or else pull over until either visibility improves or another car smashes into them. The Contemplatives ask God to see them through the storm, without too many niggling questions about who sent the storm in the first place. Saint Christopher is the patron saint of travelers, and this is the reason he's on the dashboard—not to hang leftover Mardi Gras beads.

Then there's my friend Russ. When he takes the wheel in a storm, I'm surprised a roustabout doesn't confirm that passengers are at least five feet tall and ask for their tickets. At the end of the ride, God willing, they expect to be able to buy a loganberry and a sugar waffle.

So forget about whether your intended caps the tooth-paste or not. *Never* marry anyone without first having them drive you through a storm. The only ongoing argument that causes more divorces is over the thermostat.

Which brings us to the larger question: why would any sane person *want* storm stories in the first place, especially if one is not writing screenplays for Hollywood catastrophe films? Because storms make for the best memories. Think of all those holidays where you strove to buy the greatest gifts, make the perfect pudding, find the most amazing outfit— and yet the photos all seem the same. The holidays we most vividly recall are those spent eating Christmas dinner out of an airport vending machine, when Grandpa put the moves on one of Santa's helpers at the mall, how the cat toppled over a lit menorah, the dog stole the roast, and the sewer backed up. To paraphrase John Lennon, storms are what happen to you while you're busy making other plans.

Ridin' on the Thruway

As riots and deteriorating conditions in the city sent people fleeing to the suburbs, we became entranced by lawns and briquettes and also slaves to the automobile, even before they had cup holders. Good-bye city buses. With coffee and coins in hand, we took to the open road in DeSotos with soaring tailfins and rocketlike thruster lamps that were poised for takeoff.

However, the New York Thruway wasn't destined to become the setting for fast action car-chase movies like *Thunder Road*, *Grand Theft Auto*, *Smokey and the Bandit*, or *The Cannonball Run*. There'd be no chart-topping rhythm and blues song called "Get Your Kicks on the Governor Thomas E. Dewey Thruway." It was not a meeting place for John Lennon and Paul McCartney that would become immortalized as the tuneful "Penny Lane."

Built in the 1950s, the 641-mile Thruway is the longest toll highway in the United States. It runs north from New York City to Albany, where you can continue northward to Montreal or make a left turn toward Buffalo. An hour west of Rochester you see the welcome sign that says Buffalo, An All America City. At first glance you assume that the Chamber of Commerce doesn't want you to mistakenly think you've arrived in an Armenian city or among the Khomani San Bushmen of the Kalahari. And then you wonder, if they wanted to brag, why not just say, "Hey, we're not Cleveland." But it turns out that the prestigious All-America City designation is awarded by the National Civic League to places that have demonstrated a spirit of cooperation and creativity in solving community challenges.

From Buffalo, the Thruway heads southwest to the

Pennsylvania border. It also connects to four bridges over the Niagara River and from there to highways leading to Toronto and Cleveland. In the east, the Thruway seamlessly connects to the highway systems of New Jersey, Massachusetts, and Connecticut. There are no dangerous curves or steep hills, intersections, or traffic lights, and billboards are kept to a minimum. It's quite unlike I-95 in that no one is flipping you the bird, flashing their headlights at you, or honking the horn and tailgating. You don't have to suffer through enormous signs speculating if your teen is on drugs, if you need depression medication, or both. Ambulances don't regularly roar past, and by the side of the road you don't see many blood-soaked passengers on gurneys. However, there's the occasional bovine strolling along the shoulder, making you wonder if instead of heading for Niagara Falls you may be on the Grand Trunk Road in northern India. Holy cow!

This is not to say that people don't speed and state troopers don't catch them, along with the lost cows. They lurk behind trees and around curves, both troopers and heifers. And girls, don't bother telling no-nonsense New York state troopers that you're pregnant and needed a restroom. They don't care if you pee in a cup, wear an adult diaper, or wet yourself. Being with child, in fact, is another very good reason to slow down! New Jersey troopers, on the other hand, are much more sympathetic to this situation. Just be prepared for a police escort to the nearest lavatory.

Though it looks appealingly Euclidean, the Thruway wasn't a mathematician's dream but a product of topography. It runs up the Hudson Valley to the Mohawk Valley and into the Great Lakes region to avoid mountain systems created millions of years ago and finished off by glaciers during the last ice age. Speaking of ice ages, as good a road as the Thruway is, you don't want to be driving on it during a blizzard. This is where the idea for the show *Ice Road Truckers* originated.

People like to try and pinpoint the decline of Buffalo, and the top three culprits are usually (1) moving manufacturing overseas; (2) the opening of the Saint Lawrence Seaway in 1959, bypassing the Erie Canal; and (3) the building of the Kensington and Scajaquada expressways broke up a number of East Side neighborhoods.

In the early fifties, it was thought that an east–west highway within the city that would link the new suburbs and make the airport convenient to downtown would be just the ticket. However, the Scajaquada destroyed a park and the Kensington a thriving Jewish and German neighborhood called Humboldt Park that was quickly becoming African American. Construction went predominantly unopposed since the residents leaving didn't care and the ones arriving didn't have any political clout. Perhaps the ultimate irony is that the park and the Kensington have been renamed after Martin Luther King Jr.

Obviously the contractors didn't go to the University at Buffalo School of Engineering and Applied Sciences, since they hit bedrock and went bankrupt. As a court reporter, my dad had to listen to this lawsuit every day for years, and when he drives the Kensington all he can think of is typing hundreds of thousands of pages of boring transcripts. In fact, he can't even watch *The Flintstones* because it takes place in Bedrock.

Loss of Critical Mass: When the Saints Go Marching Out

Mark Twain once said that you can't throw a brick in Montreal without breaking a church window. The same is true for Buffalo if you add saloon windows. But it won't be the case much longer at the rate churches are closing. Fortunately, the bars are still safe as best I can tell. And the two seem to coexist quite peacefully. In fact, on Washington Street there's a Catholic Charities office just two doors away from alternative rock bar Club Diablo, which features bands such as Stigma and Morgue Riot.

The Catholics of the nineteenth century paid, prayed, and obeyed, but the size of the American flock began declining in the late twentieth century, coinciding with the rising number of just-on-Sunday Catholics (and just-in-case Catholics), who don't send their children to parochial school, religion class, or Catholic Youth Organization.

Western New York is no longer 80 percent Catholic, the way it was when I was growing up, chock-full of Irish, Polish, and Italian immigrants, with each family hoping to produce a priest. Buffalo's professionally dominant Germans, who made up half the area population in 1900, were divided between Catholic and Protestant (usually Lutheran). When I was born, in 1965, one-third of all Buffalo schoolchildren attended parochial schools, while 3,300 habit-covered nuns kept the area safe from the ravages of chewing gum. Now, enrollment is just 15 percent and dropping like the mercury in March, while only 950 nuns remain, many of whom are in infirmaries. Apparently, joining a convent has become about as popular as enrolling in finishing school, possibly as a result of the lure of that other Madonna, even though modernization has meant that few sisters still don habits, and it transpires that many nuns do in fact have hair, along with those other body parts we weren't sure about.

On the ecumenical streets of Buffalo there's really no way to identify Catholics since they don't sport yarmulkes or head scarves, or put I Support Non-Prophet Organizations bumper stickers on their hybrids the way Unitarians do. But there is an audio cue—they'll automatically say, "God rest his soul" after the mention of any dead person, or one who has "put on his heavenly armor," in local parlance. When I was growing up there were also a number of telltale signs in the home, including de rigueur crucifixes and washed-out watercolors of the Virgin Mary. The classic Italian living room usually contained plastic-covered purple sofas, ridiculously light-colored shag carpeting, and possibly a fountain. No one was allowed in there because it was being saved for a visit by the pope. If a ball rolled into sanctum sanctorum, you had to crawl on your knees with your feet up, as if decommissioning a bomb. You got in and out as fast and carefully as possible, all while Nonna was in the basement kitchen using the home meat slicer on the pancetta and whipping up a batch of sauce.

Still, decades of heavy-duty Catholicism has left behind a rich legacy. "Bingo arms" or "Bingo wings" refers to upper-arm flab on great aunts who can make your ears pop from the change in pressure when they hug you. The ever popular "offer it up" continues to suggest that one embrace the bad along with the good, since celestial points will be gained for sacrifice to God. When I was in school, gym teachers enjoyed applying this panacea to most bruises, abrasions, and hurt feelings. Mothers saved it for when children didn't get their way or complained about doing chores. One also still hears expressions of surprise or dismay that have Jesus doing various aerobic activities, such as "Jesus Christ on roller skates!" "Jesus Christ on a pogo stick!" and "Jesus Christ hanging from the cross!" Under similar circumstances, Jesus was also given a middle initial, as in "Jesus H. Christ!" According to Wikipedia, the *H* most likely stands for Harold (as in, "Harold Be Thy Name"?), which you'd probably already guessed. Best of all, we've been left to parse, deconstruct, and play backward Led Zeppelin's "Stairway to Heaven," wherein the line, "To be a rock and not to roll," clearly references Saint Peter and the founding of the church.

Since its restructuring effort began in 2005, the Diocese of Buffalo has sold about a third of the seventy-seven worship sites closed or slated to close. Seven former Catholic churches are now used by other religious groups, a few have been turned into museums, several are being converted into living spaces, and Saint Gerard's is scheduled to move south to Georgia. Honestly, it's not hard to see how after months of the temperature hovering near zero with a windchill of ten below, a blistering sermon on the fires of hell isn't going to attract a big crowd. If anything, it's an appealing travel brochure, although I don't think anyone expected an entire church to pack up its pews, bells, and basilica and relocate to the Sunbelt.

The church is looking into other cutbacks as well. In the same way that scientists recently whacked Pluto off the planetary list, there's talk of closing the doors on limbo (Latin for "the edge of hell"). Limbo is the place where, once installed, you're not subject to further suffering, as opposed to purgatory, which involves continuous suffering and is in no danger of closing its doors anytime soon. Perhaps a merger could save limbo. I know that the Catholic Church and the Academy of Sciences haven't always seen eye to eye on the issues of the day, but this could be an opportunity for both to reach out and smooth over that whole Galileo business once and for all. Limbo is hot, hot, hot and Pluto is cold, cold, cold. You see where I'm going with this—celestial real estate with no-money-down eternal mortgages. Because we can't just stand by and let limbo go. Next it will be the conga and then the rumba and finally the macarena, which reminds me of a poem: "When the pope came for the limbo, I remained silent; I did not do the limbo," etc.

Still, there's the rip-roaring Irish Festival every August, complete with fiddles, tin whistles, Uilleann pipes, theatricals, baby-kissing politicians, potato chowder, plenty of brown bottles, and Sunday morning Mass. Likewise, Buffalo is home to the country's largest Saint Patrick's Day parade west of Manhattan. What the ripsnorting celebration lacks in sobriety it more than makes up for in society, confirmed by the boomlet of wee Conors and Mary Catherines that miraculously arrive right around Christmastime. Saints be praised!

And you can always find a handmade butter lamb for Easter at the famous Broadway market, along with fried Polish angel wings cookies, also known as chruściki. Buffalo now has the largest Dyngus Day parade in the world. For those leading deprived secular lives, Dyngus Day is Easter Monday and marks the end of Lent, forty days of prayer and abstinence between Ash Wednesday and Easter Sunday. Dyngus Day festivities involve squirting people with water, an ancient purification rite, and if you've ever seen how clean the garage of an Old World Pole is, then you know they're not kidding. It also involves consuming copious amounts of Tyskie beer and pierogi pizza and listening to the polka version of Rick James's "Super Freak."

A hop-step and a close-step leads us to the Buffalo chapter of Polkaholics Anonymous. Some people might have seen Gary Larson's *Far Side* cartoon with the dialogue "Welcome to heaven, here's your harp. Welcome to hell, here's your accordion." Or heard the definition of an optimist: an accordion player with a pager. Or followed this fail-proof safety guideline: hide all of your valuables inside an accordion case.

The polka originated in central Europe in the mid-nineteenth century and was brought to Buffalo by immigrants, along with kielbasa, golabki, babka, beet borscht, and sauerkraut soup. However, it wasn't the national dance of Poland, and so the question is, why did it remain popular and not go the way of the gavotte? I think the answer says a lot about why local communities have remained close-knit and egalitarian. The effervescent polka is for all ages and all levels of ability, the band takes almost every request (yes, they know "Who Stole the Kishka?"), the musicians also like to dance (and are usually very good), a wide variety of clothing is acceptable (may I turn your attention to the cowboy fringe and the checkered hat?), individual dance styles are welcome, special occasions such as birthdays and anniversaries are always announced, and the musicians almost all have day jobs. As for the polka-dot pattern, it was indeed named after the polka, when the dance swept London in the late 1800s, but there's no further connection unless a designer danced too many "Beer Barrel Polkas" and began to see spots.

As a direct insult to Buffalo, the hip-hop-favoring high priests of the Grammy Awards eliminated the category for best polka album in 2009. Over the decades, a number of local squeeze box and tuba-toting musicians had been nominated for the coveted statuette. It's hard not to suspect that *Forbes* magazine wasn't behind this added indignity.

Growing up in Buffalo in the sixties and seventies there were manifold benefits to having plenty of Catholic friends, because *church* was also a verb that offered a wide range of parties and activities, or a "grand funferall," as James Joyce might say. They also had terrific holidays. Sorry, Jews, but atonement and fasting are just not that appealing to a child, especially one who worships milk chocolate. Best of all was that the Catholic Church conveniently issued lists of banned books and records, thereby vastly simplifying the search to learn what was cool. Since this was before computers, the church was the most reliable way to find out when a new George Carlin or Richard Pryor album was arriving in stores. Seeing as how the pope recently denounced the Harry Potter books, it would appear that this system is still in good working order, in case you don't have time to read reviews. My Unitarian church didn't provide a reading list per se, but they were always nattering on about Emerson and Darwin and Thoreau, which, to a ten-year-old, was about as exciting as watching Walden Pond freeze over.

What is the religious mix in Buffalo today? Everything. Immigrants from all parts of the globe enrich local culture with their traditions, celebrations, and miraculous soccer skills.

Increase the Peace

I was raised in the Unitarian Universalist Church of Amherst, which was created in 1960 by adding a chapel onto an existing mansion. The mostly glass chapel provided a wonderful atmosphere to reflect on nature, and in wintertime its low-slung eaves produced weapons-grade icicles for kids to joust with.

The Unitarians are derived from Christianity, since we believe in one God, more or less. If you think that LGBT is a sandwich, then you're probably not Unitarian. We're the weak-tea sister to the Methodists, who are the weak-tea sisters to the Presbyterians, and so on up Jacob's Ladder until you get to the Evangelicals. We like to say that our spiritual life involves a responsible search for truth and meaning, which largely involves reading the liberal *New York Times* while asking ourselves, "But is it good for the UUs?"

The first Unitarian church in Buffalo was built on Franklin at Eagle Street by Benjamin Rathbun in 1833. This Buffalo native erected hundreds of buildings in the area, including hotels, businesses, taverns, residences, and even the city jail. After becoming overextended and forging notes, or kiting checks, in today's parlance, the master builder was arrested in 1836 and had to be tried in Batavia because he was so popular locally. While awaiting his day in court, Rathbun was incarcerated in the very jail he'd built for the city of Buffalo. He eventually spent five years in the Big House, a.k.a Auburn Prison. In 1957, a document was found that suggested Rathbun's brother, Lyman, may have been ultimately responsible for the fraud.

The English Gothic–style Buffalo Unitarian Church on Elmwood Avenue at West Ferry Street that we know today was built by Edward Austin Kent in 1904. It was most likely his last work before going down on the *Titanic*, and he's buried in Forest Lawn Cemetery. Kent was the only Buffalonian to lose his life when, on April 15, 1912, the ship rammed an iceberg off the coast of Newfoundland and sank. On the bright side, he was traveling first class, and he would surely be pleased to know his church is thriving, recently hosting an event featuring a band called the Bloodthirsty Vegans.

The Buffalo area is home to hundreds of beautiful and historic religious sites in addition to the previously mentioned Our Lady of Victory Basilica and National Shrine. Over two hundred of these can be viewed in a photo gallery by Karl R. Josker at www.pbase.com/kjosker/churches. When checking them out in person, one does not want to miss Blessed Trinity, which is considered to be one of the most masterful reproductions in the United States of the twelfth-century Lombard-Romanesque style of architecture. Same with Westminster Presbyterian and its Tiffany windows, Corpus Christi Church, with its six large Madonnas reproduced from famous Marian shrines in Poland, Saint Louis Church, and Saint Ann's Church and Shrine.

Forty minutes to the north, in Youngstown, is Our Lady of Fatima Shrine, with its breathtaking dome basilica topped by a thirteen-foot statue of Mary. Our Lady of Fatima is the name for the Blessed Virgin Mary who appeared to three shepherd children in Portugal in 1917 and imparted three secrets to them. The first was a vision of hell, the second included a recipe to save souls from hell and convert the world to Roman Catholicism, and the third was a vision of death for Pope John Paul II and some other religious figures. In fact, Our Lady reminds me a little of my friend's Bubbe Dorothy, since she only tends to get in touch when there's bad news to impart.

In addition to the statue of Our Lady of Fatima, the magnificent site features over 150 life-size bronze and marble statues, a natural pond, and a heart-shaped rosary pool. There are daily masses and confessions along with sustenance and souvenirs for thousands of visitors. One reason for Fatima's continued popularity is that her message is known as the "Peace Plan from Heaven."

Fortunately for me, UUs can still qualify for heaven. The Vatican think tank has produced a doctrine to cope with "invincible ignorance," a sort of corollary to "papal infallibility," which basically says that if you don't know that the Catholic Church is the one true church through no fault of your own, then God will still allow you a shot at salvation. The only problem is that as nice as heaven may sound, Unitarians aren't really in favor of gated communities.

Life in Amherst

Our Amherst isn't the famous one where Emily Dickinson holed up in her white dress to scribble about hope, death, and immortality, but rather some marshland drained to create a first-ring suburb northeast of Buffalo. With a population of 116,000, the town has so far produced one *American Idol* finalist and consistently ranks as one of America's top five safest cities, based on crime statistics. But see for yourself. Some winter morning at Boulevard or Eastern Hills Mall, join the ardent power walkers in their sequined tracksuits or business attire, carrying free weights or pushing strollers, plugged into iPods or chatting with friends, and near the fountain you'll find heaps of coats, bags, umbrellas, and energy bars, all for the taking.

My good friend Mary and my mom still live within minutes of where I grew up, though my mom now goes to Florida in the winter. Mary comes from a small Catholic family of eleven people and is the youngest of nine children. (Bedrooms didn't have TVs back then.) Her house was such a piratical free-for-all of kids and pets and coups d'état that for long stretches of time I don't think anyone was Mom's favorite. With raucous games, practical jokes, and heated rivalries almost always in progress, there was excitement in the air, more than a hint of danger, and the very real possibility of a head injury. But you couldn't take a family of eleven people out anywhere in the Buffalo of the seventies, with all of its various strikes and protests, since you'd have immediately been arrested for unlawful assembly. When all was said and the battles were done at Mary's house, the life lesson learned from diving headlong into such anarchy was that in the larger scheme of things, we kids weren't so much special as replaceable.

Mary's three kids can't get away with much nonsense since she knows every dodge and how it's played—though I understand that school pranks are much more sophisticated these days. Letting a greased pig run through the halls, dropping a thousand marbles down the stairs, setting alarm clocks to go off at noon in all the lockers, placing dry ice in urinals, and putting For Sale signs on the lawns of the faculty is as passé as a Mr. Bill bobblehead. Such Paleolithic hijinks have apparently been replaced with hacking into school computers, creating controversial blogs and provocative Facebook pages, and secretly bidding against teachers on eBay during study hall.

Still, other routines remain the same. People in the Buffalo area often eat dinner between five and six o'clock, a remnant of being a factory town. After all, it's Amherst, not Argentina. Suddenly, the mall is empty but for a few dead-enders and latchkey kids. Despite whatever diet or health craze is sweeping the nation, Western New Yorkers still enjoy hearty foods like casseroles, meatloaf, chili, and lasagna. The body's internal pipes are viewed the same way as the ones inside your home—they need to be lined in order to keep from freezing. Substantive meals also contribute to the congeniality of the population. People who dine strictly on chopped salads, Soyjoys, and celery stalks are tired, cold, and hungry all of the time and tend to be irritable. Ask any rancher: in a blizzard, it's always the undernourished that fall away from the herd.

Our storybook Main Street, which goes from downtown Buffalo through cloverleafy Amherst, has been under construction since before I was born, and locals like to say it's how you can tell that a Democrat is mayor. Over the past forty years, Amherst has been home to a certain amount of urban sprawl involving office parks, big box stores, chain restaurants, and displaced deer, all of which have caused other towns to put laws on their books specifically intended to prevent them from "becoming like Amherst." That said, having the University at Buffalo's North Campus in the backyard offers local residents beautifully appointed hiking and biking trails, along with easy access to numerous lectures, sporting events, films, concerts, theater, and dance. And some good grazing for the deer. When it comes to grazing for bipeds, you can't beat nearby Duff's, on Sheridan Drive, where they make wings hot, serve beer cold, and stay open late. The suburban eatery recently edged out Buffalo's famed Anchor Bar as "Lord of the Wings" in an episode of the Travel Channel's *Food Wars.*

Amherst is just large enough to require left-hand turn signals at major intersections, but not so big that my mom can't listen to the police scanner and match up the addresses with people she knows. However, I still use my Amherst address on my driver's license since the Manhattan DMV is Dante's ninth circle of hell. Mom loves to call and give dramatic readings of the letters accompanying my speeding tickets that start with, "Driving is a privilege, not a right."

The Best-Kept Secret

When I was growing up in the seventies, there was no diagnosis of attention deficit disorder. The more kindly teachers said you were energetic, while the others jotted down "behavioral problems." My brain was like a television set with 100 channels (an anachronism since we only had four at the time) continuously flipping to the next show. Somehow I discovered that high doses of sugar helped reduce this frantic state of mind. At the time it didn't make sense that a stimulant could help calm down overstimulation, but then I don't understand how Ritalin, also a stimulant, is supposed to help ADHD. Anyway, it worked, and so I had something called sponge candy squirreled away in my locker and desk drawers. My sponge habit had no side effects, other than some rascally mice occasionally helping themselves to my stash and perhaps a bit of acne.

Most Buffalonians don't know a MoonPie from a bear claw. But sponge candy—carmelized sugar with spun molasses surrounded by milk or dark chocolate—thrives in cool, overcast weather (not unlike silverfish) and makes up the top layer of the Buffalo food pyramid, right between chicken wings and beef on weck (thinly sliced rare roast beef and horseradish sauce on kummelweck—a roll topped with kosher salt and caraway seeds), but without the international notoriety. Sponge candy is inside information, what you learn from actually living in the Buffalo area, like how to turn the wheel into a skid on an icy road. People say Buffalo's best-kept secret is the gorgeous summer weather, but it's actually sponge candy. You can find it everywhere (even in the supermarket bulk bins) in the Sponge Triangle, which reaches from Rochester, New York, in the east to Erie, Pennsylvania, in the west, but pretty much disappears beyond there. By the time you reach Albany or Pittsburgh or Cleveland, you're out of sponge range. A few isolated places around the country claim to make it under names like sponge taffy, cinderblock, sea foam, molasses puffs, honeycomb, and fairy food, but it's like eating Buffalo wings or pizza outside of Buffalo, and who are they kidding?

You can find terrific sponge candy at any local candy shop, including Fowler's, Watson's, Sweet Tooth, Aléthea's, Bella Mia, Antoinette's, Condrell's, Oliver's, Platter's, Yia Yia's Goodies, Ko-Ed, and Park Edge Sweets. Trust me, I've tried them all. And at Easter time, most carry chocolate bowling balls and bowling pins! Grocery stores and specialty food stores are hit-or-miss because sponge candy goes off once outside a narrow band of temperature (so don't put it in the freezer or take it to the beach). It also goes stale rather quickly. And if the chocolate coating flakes off and moisture gets inside, think cotton candy in a rainstorm.

My favorite sponge dealer is Parkside Candy on Main Street. Around since 1927, this old-time soda fountain is now like a crumbling French château, complete with the original mirrored mahogany doors and windows. Another Parkside location was so reliably unrenovated that scenes for the 1930s-era movie *The Natural* were filmed there in 1983. I was originally in the film but ended up on the cutting-room floor, probably because I accidentally rode through on my ten-speed Takara bicycle while wearing a Walkman blaring "Message In a Bottle" by The Police and was oblivious to the classic cars lining the street and the film crew frantically waving their arms at me. But honestly, who'd ever heard of a movie being shot in Buffalo? People turned out in droves to watch filming and to catch a glimpse of Robert Redford. As a result, there was no shortage of volunteers to be extras. I just wasn't one of them.

More recently, Keanu Reeves was in town for the movie *Henry's Crime*, in which he plays a toll taker involved in a bank heist. The plot requires a Prohibition tunnel, which makes Buffalo the perfect location. Over the years the city has been called "snowy" and "damp" and even "dreary," but *never* "dry." When asked his opinion on what is the best part of Buffalo, Reeves replied, "The people."

Nowadays I like to sit in the romantic alcove booth in the back of Parkside Candy, where it's easy to imagine people coming in for a fifteen-cent sandwich and paying ten cents for a twelve-ounce Coke during the Great Depression, when waitstaff made fifteen cents an hour and tips were rare. Or during the fifties, when Buffalo was in its rock-around-the-clock heyday, and on a Saturday night teenage boys with duck's ass hairdos brought in girls wearing poodle skirts and cardigan sweaters for sodas and sundaes. Although the licorice pipes and chocolate cigars are long gone, in addition to their sponge candy and other confections Parkside still has pecan dixies and wonderful old-fashioned homemade lollipops in flavors like Irish cream, peach schnapps, and piña colada. I'm thinking that if you're trying to make it from a three-martini lunch to happy hour, the lollipops might work along the lines of a nicotine patch and tide you over.

There's an old, worn booklet about the founding of Parkside that the waitresses will let you see if you ask for it. It's the only remaining copy, and in New York City they'd have it enclosed in a glass case instead of allowing it to be passed around while sticky-fingered customers down parfaits and tin roof sundaes. The text insists the employees are so happy and contented because of all the light and air in the factory adjacent to the restaurant. I especially like to read that part aloud to the staff.

Although *Buffalo* and *beer* can often be found in the same sentence, we have another highly esteemed local libation:

loganberry. Much like Buffalonians themselves, loganberries are sturdy and resistant to frost and disease. And like many Buffalo children, this concoction was developed by accident, when lawyer and horticulturist James Harvey Logan was crossing berry plants in his Santa Cruz, California, garden. In the late 1800s, loganberry juice went on sale at Crystal Beach, a popular amusement park and summer resort across the Niagara River in Ontario, Canada, and has been a regional specialty ever since.

Other local favorites are fried bologna and onion sandwiches, and a fish fry where the beer-batter-laden haddock hangs off the edge of the plate. When it's accompanied by a generous helping of glistening French fries, you can almost hear your arteries snapping shut as the plates hit the table. Although standards for Catholics have been relaxed with regard to not eating meat on Fridays (the day Christ died, so one refrains from blood-based entrees), the fish fry is still a popular practice in Buffalo as dictated by the Bible, in Paul's letter to Mrs. Paul. What's not in the Bible, or apparently any grammar book, for that matter, is whether a plurality of these events should be advertised as "Fish Frys" or "Fish Fries."

At the Taste of Buffalo festival, one can sample ethnic fare from Afghanistan to Venezuela. It's the second-largest food festival in the United States after Taste of Chicago, with over 450,000 people enjoying fun and foodstuffs by the forklift. Delicacies include barbecued spaghetti, roast beef sundaes, and beer-cheese soup. Check, please. If you're not in a carb coma by then, get ready for the annual Sorrento Cheese Italian Heritage Festival, which usually runs the following weekend on Hertel Avenue in North Buffalo's Little Italy. Devout Pastafarians won't go away hungry or disappointed. Fortunately, it's possible to work off a few calories by building cheese sculptures and playing in the bocce ball tournament.

Labor Day weekend brings the National Buffalo Wing Festival, with over a hundred varieties of chicken wings, including garlic parmesan, Cajun barbecue, and Thai chili, along with competitions such as the US Chicken Wing Eating Championship, various sauce-offs, the Blue Cheese Bowl (bobbing for wings), and the grueling .5K Chicken Wing Run. In an example of life imitating art, Buffalonian Drew "The Wing King" Cerza got the idea from *Osmosis Jones*, a movie that stars Bill Murray as an indiscriminate eater training to attend the Super Bowl of junk food, the National Buffalo Wing Festival. A rip-roaring success since its founding, in 2002, one wing has led to another and now there's also a National Buffalo Wing Hall of Flame and Cluckers for Cash promotion. Hollywood thought the joke was on Buffalo, but the film lost money, whereas this wingding of a festival attracts thousands of out-of-towners and pours lots of cash into local coffers in addition to raising funds for several charities.

Gone but not forgotten is the locally owned and operated Freddie's Donuts, which had the best glazed donuts from the 1930s through the 1980s. When Krispy Kreme arrived in Manhattan in the late 1990s, Buffalo expats phoned one another and yelled, "Freddie's Donuts!" We ran. Or took the subway. They weren't *as* good, but close. And rumors continue to swirl that the Krispy Kreme secret recipe was purchased (or stolen!) from local proprietor Freddie Maier.

One can still get great donuts at places like Paula's, home of the celebrated Texas donut, Dickie's, Famous Doughnuts, and Russ's—and Budwey's makes a mean apple fritter—but it sure was sad when they recently tore old Freddie's down. Nothing said quadruple bypass quite like a dozen Freddie's hot glazed donuts in the maroon-and-white box.

Let's Go, Buffalo!

The universal Buffalo sport, or maybe it's more of a dance step, is the flamingo. This is where you stand on one foot while yanking on or off your boots. It's easy to spot Buffalonians and other Snowbelters in airports—people of all ages, shapes, and sizes deftly removing shoes while holding luggage without needing to sit down or even balance against the metal detector. It's an acquired skill, like thumping bricks of greasy black snow off from underneath the car without getting your shoes or pant legs dirty.

The Buffalo News (one of the few profitable papers in the country!) has oft been criticized by the intelligentsia for having a daily sports section, but not a daily arts section. As Judy Garland said about singing "Over the Rainbow" for the umpteenth time, "Give the people what they want and then go out and get a hamburger." Well, Buffalonians are ballpark-frank-carrying don't-cry-for-me-Buffalo-Sabres to-the bleacher-born wild about their teams.

Buffalo was one of the first American cities to have a pro baseball team, which began playing on August 3, 1877. In their many incarnations, the Buffalo Bisons are one of the most senior teams in baseball history. The minor-league Bisons play to good crowds in the downtown Coca-Cola Field, but the hope of major-league baseball coming to the city is right up there with a Bass Pro shop moving in and the Virgin Mary appearing on Lake Erie. It's the Buffalo version of fantasy baseball.

War Memorial, better known as "The Rockpile," a demolished stadium where the Bisons and Bills used to play, was employed to depict a major-league stadium from the 1930s in filming the 1984 Robert Redford baseball movie,

The Natural. It wasn't much of a stretch since the downtown
Buffalo stadium had been a Works Progress Administration
project, constructed between 1935 and 1937 under President Franklin D. Roosevelt's New Deal. However, the once
majestic edifice was poorly maintained, and sportswriter
Brock Yates said that in later years the stadium "looks as if
whatever war it was a memorial to had been fought within
its confines."

From 1970 to 1978, the city was home to the short-
lived Buffalo Braves basketball team, now the Los Angeles
Clippers. Likewise, two similarly ephemeral soccer teams,
the Buffalo Stallions (1979–1984) and the Buffalo Blizzards
(1992–2001), both indoor leagues (for obvious reasons),
briefly kicked the ball around town. The Buffalo Bandits
have been playing lacrosse since 1992, with encouragement
from their whimsically named cheerleaders, the Bandettes.

Daniel Patrick Moynihan, four-time New York Democratic senator and big Buffalo Bills fan, once said, "I don't
think there's any point in being Irish if you don't know
that the world is going to break your heart eventually." He
could've been talking about his favorite team. Or, as one
local T-shirt proclaims, Buffalo is a drinking town with a
football problem.

No, Buffalo's football team is not named the Bills in
honor of all the exorbitant heating bills local residents receive
every winter, or for the number of repo men wandering its
streets, or for the fact that we're currently the debt-collection
capital of the country. "The Bills" was the winning entry in a
local contest, which named the team after the Buffalo Bills,
a football franchise from the All-American Football Conference that merged with the Cleveland Browns back in 1950.
That team was named after William Frederick "Buffalo Bill"
Cody. The Bills' cheerleaders are known as the Buffalo Jills,
and the mascot is Billy Buffalo.

In September of 1962, the Buffalo Bills claimed future congressman Jack Kemp (1935–2009) for a $100 waiver fee in what's been called one of the biggest bargains in professional football history. Kemp completed twenty-one of thirty-five passes for 230 yards and two touchdowns in his very first game before delighted fans carried him off the field.

Buffalo is the only team to win four consecutive American Football Conference Championships and lose four consecutive Super Bowls. The most legendary moment and moniker in Bills history comes from Scott Norwood's missed kick in 1991's Super Bowl XXV against the New York Giants, famously noted as "wide right."

Oddly enough, this incident became a plot point in the 1998 hipster movie *Buffalo '66*, about a guy born during a championship Bills game (forcing his mother, a die-hard fan, to miss the blessed event). As a young adult, Billy (of course) places $10,000 on the Bills in a Super Bowl game that's lost by a player named Scott Wood missing the winning field goal. Angry Billy winds up in prison after taking the rap for a crime he didn't commit in order to repay his bookie, and upon release he wants to murder the Bills kicker. Buffalo comes across as a gritty working-class city with slab concrete buildings and corner saloons cemented in the seventies. Meantime, Billy's love interest appears to have self-esteem so low that the battered women's shelter is holding a cot with her name on it.

The team was also part of one of the most controversial episodes in NFL history, known as the catchy "Music City Miracle." Late in the fourth quarter of a wild card playoff game against the Tennessee Titans in Nashville on January 8, 2000, Titans tight end Frank Wycheck fielded a kickoff and threw what appeared to be an illegal forward pass to Titan Kevin Dyson, who ran down the sidelines for a seventy-five-yard touchdown. Following a long official review, the touchdown ruling was upheld and the Titans won the game 22–16.

A year after a famous 2007 end zone fight following a game against the Cincinnati Bengals, *The Wall Street Journal* anointed Buffalo Bills fans as some of the most irrationally exuberant in all of sports history. Well, those weren't the exact words they used. On the bright side, a *Sports Illustrated* survey ranked them first in tailgating and about sixth in fan IQ. Buffalonians are quick to point out that some rabble-rousing must be attributed to the 15 to 20 percent omnibibulous Canadian turnout who like to get started early when it comes to team spirits. A popular tailgate breakfast is kegs and eggs followed by roasting a pig on a spit and bowling-ball shots (yes, these involve a real bowling ball, but you can wear your own shoes).

In January 2008, the Bills became the only American football team to play annual home games outside the United States by moving one of its games for each of the next five years to the Rogers Centre in Toronto, Ontario. In 2009, they celebrated their fiftieth anniversary to great local fanfare, complete with the Bills logo appearing on Labatt's beer sold in New York State. However, the team enjoyed only one winning season in the past ten years, which has resulted in the usual round of jokes. WBFO radio host Bert Gambini told me, "I had two Bills tickets on my dashboard when I stopped in at the store. When I came out, the windshield was smashed and there were two more."

Making an infinite loop on the Internet you'll find:

Q. What do the Buffalo Bills and Billy Graham have in common?
A. Both can get 70,000 people on their feet yelling, "Jesus Christ!"

Q. How many Buffalo Bills does it take to win a Super Bowl?
A. Nobody knows, and we may never find out.

Still, they've managed to put Buffalo on the map in another way. Bills receiver Terrell Owens had a seven-episode VH1 reality series called *The T.O. Show*. How could visitors not be attracted to lines like "Get your fur underwear out because it's going to be cold." If locals decide to purchase a pair of his $137,000 asteroid-sized diamond earrings to go with said ermine undies, not only will it do wonders for the economy but we can save energy by turning down the streetlights at night. Even though Owens didn't take the Bills to the play-offs, after his one-year contract expired, fans didn't ask him to leave his copy of the key to the city in his mailbox on the way out.

Win or lose, snow or shine, members of Bills Backers, a Buffalo Bills fan club with 330 chapters in all fifty states and twelve countries, gather together in their local bars, restaurants, and community centers around the world to support their favorite team on game days.

The Buffalo Sabres ice hockey team joined the National Hockey League in the 1970–71 season and were also the product of a name-the-team contest. Previously, the Buffalo Bisons were an American Hockey League franchise that played in the city from 1940 to 1970 and became Calder Cup champs in 1943, 1944, 1946, 1963, and 1970. Despite twenty-eight trips to the play-offs, the Sabres have never taken home the Stanley Cup. However, in 1973, when they lost to the Montreal Canadiens in game six in Buffalo, the night memorably concluded with grateful fans chanting, "Thank you, Sabres!"

The "wide right" equivalent for Buffalo hockey is "in the crease" or "no goal" and was deemed by ESPN as the worst call in sports history, made during the 1999 Stanley Cup finals between the Sabres and the Dallas Stars. In front of each goal there's a goal crease surrounded by thin red lines and filled in with light blue. At the time, it was illegal to score a goal if an offensive player's skate entered the crease before the puck did. During the sixth game, Dallas Stars winger Brett Hull scored a triple-overtime goal with his skate clearly in the crease (but the puck was not) and ended the series, with the Stars taking the cup. This was most certainly the inspiration for a T-shirt that says Buffalo Hockey—Un-Puck'n Believable.

Mike Harrington, longtime *Buffalo News* sports reporter and columnist (and classmate of mine at Sweet Home High School) takes a Dickensian approach in summing up fandom. "Is this the best time in ages to be a Buffalo sports fan? Or is it the worst? Depends on your view. The Bills and Sabres are struggling to put winning products together but they've never been better at putting together the *experience* of going to the game rather than staying home on your couch."

There's not a lot of armadillo racing in Buffalo, or rodeo, unless you include a few holdouts still driving Isuzu Rodeos, long rumored to be chick cars, with wider berths to accommodate "the cake effect." But you'll find no such softies in my favorite local sports league, the Queen City Roller Girls, who engage in full-contact roller derby. They can pack a rink to fire-hazard proportions with their porn-star personas and WrestleMania maneuvers, such as "bootie blocks," which involve pushing a butt up in the jammer's face, and I won't even get started on "whips." Launched in 2006 with three self-proclaimed "radical, free-thinking, free-wheeling women who love the smell of the rink and the feel of eight wheels under their feet," QCRG now numbers more than 120 women on five teams—the Suicidal Saucies, the Nickel City KnockOuts, the Devil Dollies, the Lake Effect

Furies, and the Alley Kats. Halftime means a live rock band and dozens of loaves of Al Cohen's seeded rye bread being energetically tossed into the crowd. The leaning-forward-in-our-seats evening concludes with a raffle, oftentimes a crash couch donated by the local FWS. Following one particularly vicious bout, a number of bad asses had their heads shaved to benefit Buffalo's Roswell Park Cancer Institute. Be sure to pick up a program, which, in addition to listing the rules and participants, encourages "clever shouts" and warns against yelling something stupid such as, "Nice tits, ladies!" which could obviously be harmful to your health.

When I eventually form my roller derby team, the Sweet Home Sweat Hags, we'll need some kick-ass names to match our moves. I considered going with Lunachick, but Mia Psycho's Roller Derby Name Generator, found online, had other ideas. She's got me down as Slaughter Pestilential, which for a vegetarian with seasonal allergies sounds positively harmful.

Connecting the Drops

Yes, there is a Buffalo Yacht Club. Only there aren't any yachts. It's more like the Buffalo Sailboat and Two Cabin Cruisers Club. Still, formed in 1860, The BYC is the third-oldest yacht club in America, with quality boating facilities in both the United States and Canada, thereby having the added cachet of being an *international* yacht club. But size doesn't matter (please relay that to *Forbes* magazine when they're discussing our incredible shrinking population), and despite the relatively short season, locals love being on the water. You needn't join any club to enjoy the waterfront's fabulous views, picturesque pathways, ice cream gazebo, clam bar, and restaurants. It's an ideal place to spend time whether you're a sailor, diner, picnicker, sunbather, or just in the mood for a stroll.

Of such strategic importance are the chain of five inland Great Lakes—Huron, Ontario, Michigan, Erie, and Superior—that control over them has been fought for by the British, the French, the Americans, the Indians, and even the Confederates during the Civil War.

The Iroquois called it Erie Tejocharonting, later shortened to just Erie by Franciscan friars, and it was the last Great Lake to be discovered by white men. Lake Erie is the second smallest by surface area, and the shallowest, thereby making it the most treacherous—home to the largest storms that kick up in the least amount of time, and thus a graveyard for ships and their sailors. It's also home to a large number of ice-fishing mishaps, although a number of those can be attributed to excess beer and human error rather than weather conditions. (Technically, I do not consider fishing a sport since, like hunting, the other side is unaware that they're engaged in a competition.)

Warm southern air masses collide with cold fronts

coming down from the Arctic to produce gale-force winds, waves of legendary might, and even waterspouts—funnel-shaped columns of air and spray, basically water tornadoes. Lake Erie is also the most likely to freeze, enabling a wall of snow to blow across the surface unimpeded, the way it did during the Blizzard of '77. When I was growing up, WKBW radio personality Stan Roberts used to give the daily weather report for "Lake Dreary."

Going back in time, Lake Erie is most famous as the battleground where the United States dealt a devastating blow to Great Britain's Royal Navy during the War of 1812, a turning point that was to ensure American control of the lake. The Battle of Lake Erie also gave Master Commandant Oliver Hazard Perry occasion to hoist the famous flag that read "Don't Give Up the Ship," and then scribble his legendary message on the back of an old envelope—"Dear General: We have met the enemy and they are ours. Two ships, two brigs, and one schooner."

The Barbary Coast and Somalia have nothing on the Great Lakes when it comes to swashbuckling. During the nineteenth and twentieth centuries, these freshwater seas were rife with plundering. However, pirates were more likely to have wool scarves on their shoulders rather than a parrot, and because of a distinct lack of gold in the area, the booty was timber, munitions, fish, supplies, women, and liquor, though not always in that order.

The Buffalo waterfront was equally perilous, with sailors spoiling for a fight and con men seeking out marks. Taverns with heartwarming names such as Tub of Blood and Peg Leg House usually had trapdoors leading to a room where suckers were served drugged drinks, robbed, and then rolled down a slide into the canal with a stone around their necks to make it look like suicide. Bottoms up!

The most complex, or perhaps convoluted, Great Lakes

character would have to be Mormon marauder James Jesse Strang (1813–1856). He crowned himself king of a breakaway Mormon sect, then claimed Beaver Island in Lake Michigan to be a separate country from the United States and his subjects its citizens. Passing ships were raided, the men murdered, and the women taken captive. While Strang became the only (self-appointed) monarch in US history to actually control shipping lanes, the government cried treason.

In addition to piracy, Strang practiced polygamy and animal sacrifice. All that was left was to run for public office, so he campaigned for and won a seat in the Michigan state legislature as a Democrat in 1853. Strang was reelected in 1855, but his term was cut short upon his being assassinated in 1856 by malcontents among his own people, in part for his decree that female Strangites must wear bloomers.

Though Strang and other Friends of Jolly Roger were finally stopped, plenty of booty still gets smuggled into Canada today—diamonds, drugs, tobacco, firearms, and liquor. From Canada to the United States is a regular illegal flow of nonpasteurized cheese, fireworks, and prescription drugs. Best when used together! Admittedly, it doesn't make much sense that we're taking such great pains to smuggle in bottle rockets and Ambien when automatic weapons, crack, and smack are available on certain street corners in downtown Buffalo. Then there's the question of why so many idiots wait until July 1 to try and sneak fireworks across the border.

In olden days, as now, Niagara Falls has always tried to drum up business with new and exciting attractions (sadly, the Elvis Museum didn't last). On September 8, 1827, long before PETA and the SPCA were formed, a condemned double-topsail schooner called *Michigan* was decorated like a pirate ship, with fake humans tied to the masts, and sent over Horseshoe Falls to provide entertainment and, more importantly, cash for local businesses from the more than ten thousand onlookers who came to see the spectacle. To make things even more interesting, the boat was fitted out as a veritable zoo, filled with dogs and cats, two bears, two raccoons, an Arabian camel, an elk, a fox, several hawks and geese, and a swan, though accounts differ as to the exact contents of the menagerie. Many animals were caged or tied to the ship and thus were doomed. The two bears jumped free and were able to swim to Goat Island. A goose made it to shore and was rescued, probably just in time for Sunday dinner. And one assumes the more intelligent birds flew away. Had the Buffalo Zoo been around, they could have cadged a few deer.

Nowadays, entrepreneurship is mostly under control, and visiting the falls is truly breathtaking. There are public parks with spectacular vistas, nicely appointed trails along the top, a boat ride underneath, and a guided climb behind the falls. The last two attractions are very egalitarian, as nobody looks cool in a blue or yellow plastic rain poncho, not even Brad Pitt. The falls are open twenty-four hours, 365 days a year and illuminated with different colored lights every night. On Friday and Saturday nights in the summer there are fireworks. Still, you can only gape at mighty Niagara for so long, so when you're done, although there is a whole host of amusements for young and old, I recommend a visit to the nearby Butterfly Conservatory, where the free-floating luminescent creatures appear to be auditioning for sleeping-pill commercials, and cute little toads hop about.

The Niagara River, of which the falls is a part, flows north from Lake Erie to Lake Ontario and forms part of the border between the province of Ontario in Canada and New York State, thus making regulation an international affair. When people say how Richard Nixon almost single-handedly destroyed democracy, I like to throw in, "Yes, but he cleaned up the Great Lakes." Likewise, when anything untoward is said about George W. Bush, I can now say, "Yes, but he prevented large-scale diversion of water from the Great Lakes." More recently, President Obama's 2010 budget proposed $475 billion to restore the lakes, protect native species, and prevent against dangerous intruders, in particular huge Asian carp, which are as ugly as they are aggressive and jump so high that they've given boaters black eyes, broken bones, and concussions.

The Great Lakes Compact was signed into law in 2008, thereby banning the diversion of water to places outside the region and regulating large-scale water use. The legislation was prompted when, in 1998, the province of Ontario approved a proposal to take water from Lake Superior for the purpose of shipping it to Asia in a tanker. This outraged citizens across the region and highlighted the need for strong protection of the lakes, which contain 90 percent of the nation's surface freshwater and 20 percent of the world's available freshwater. In a time of global warming and climate change, when water is more valuable than oil, the agreement is a major step forward in protecting the environmental health of the area. And as a result, the three poorest cities in the nation, Detroit, Cleveland, and Buffalo, will soon be transformed into the Rust Belt Riviera, the US equivalents of Nice, Monte Carlo, and Cannes.

So buy now, while lakefront property is still available! In January of 2009, *Forbes* ranked Buffalo as the fourth-strongest housing market in the nation, although the reason behind this is that there hadn't exactly been a boom to begin with. Still, your real estate dollars go far in Western New York, where a picture-perfect four bedroom, three bathroom house with a big backyard and a bowling alley nearby can be had for under $300,000. While overextended national banks were failing or needing bailouts, Buffalo's were in good shape, making loans, and experiencing fewer foreclosures. *BusinessWeek* named it one of the top twenty communities to ride out a recession. I'll be renewing this subscription, unlike the one for that *other* business magazine.

To Be Perfectly Frank

The National Trust for Historic Preservation named Buffalo one of its 2009 Dozen Distinctive Destinations, highlighting the city's "staggering range of cultural resources as well as some of the country's most captivating architecture." Indeed, the city contains landmarks by almost every great American architect of the late nineteenth and early twentieth centuries. "The interweaving of great architecture, landscape architecture and important historic sites makes Buffalo a must-see destination," according to National Trust president Richard Moe.

Buffalo lays claim to five Frank Lloyd Wright houses. Wright (1867–1959) is considered by many to be the greatest architect of the twentieth century, with an organic style that blends locale and landscape with earth-hugging profiles and low-slung free-flowing spaces. The Darwin D. Martin House, a prairie house complex of five buildings with a new and highly inventive glass-walled visitors' pavilion designed by Toshiko Mori, is open to the public while undergoing a much-welcome renovation after the University at Buffalo installed that groovy 1960s harvest gold kitchen. The Graycliff Estate (thirty minutes away by car in Derby, New York) has been lovingly and painstakingly restored and is also open for tours.

As it happens, you'll often see the word *Wright* in conjunction with *restoration* because although he was a groundbreaking architect, his engineering left a bit to be desired, such as firm foundations, waterproof roofs, and all those other tiny touches that not only make a house a home, but also keep a building standing upright.

The volunteers at the Frank Lloyd Wright properties are nothing if not dedicated, and I'll go so far as to say devoted.

Pete and I were out joyriding one bright winter day and pulled up at Graycliff to see how the renovations were coming along, even though we knew the lakefront property wasn't open for tours at that time of year (back then—now there are winter tours). A man was locking the door on his way out, but chatted with us excitedly about the ongoing work. The next thing we knew, he was opening the house up again, turning on the lights, and taking us on the most wonderful two-hour private tour. It transpired that he lived not far from Pete's place, so Pete gave him the address and invited him to stop by sometime in the summer to see his woodland garden. The man said that he was dying of cancer and wasn't expected to live that long. It was so moving and memorable that he'd decided to share his precious time with us along with his love for the Graycliff property. I often think back to his kindness and generosity. Sadly, this story doesn't end with a joke, unless our friend beat the cancer and is still giving tours of his beloved Graycliff. That would indeed be an excellent joke.

It's possible to do drive-bys of the privately owned two-story stucco Walter V. Davidson house (locally known as "Frank Lloyd Wright on a budget") and the redbrick William R. Heath House, with its massive square porch supports and art glass windows. And this being Buffalo, it's feasible to linger outside for a long while without neighbors calling Homeland Security, especially if you hold a Perry's ice cream cone. In fact, I was standing in front of the Davidson house chatting with a group of itinerant professors when the owner, Russell J. Maxwell, came outside with two enormous Irish wolfhounds. Instead of loosing the hounds on us, we were invited in for a terrific tour and liberally basted with canine saliva. It transpired that the Irish wolfhounds had recently come off a celebrity encounter with Gerry Adams of Sinn Fein fame, but they seemed neither to suffer from dry mouth nor be at all starstruck—true Buffalonians.

The one and only mausoleum Wright designed, called Blue Sky, can be found in Forest Lawn Cemetery. It's built into the side of a hill and consists of twenty-four crypts laid out like a staircase, with two sets of twelve crypts running parallel up the hill. My friend Russ likes to tell people that as you walk up the steps they automatically play "Blue Skies" by Irving Berlin. However, this is patently untrue, or sheer mendacity, as playwright Tennessee Williams liked to say. I tried it. Twice.

The Larkin Company administration building in Buffalo, completed in 1904, was Wright's first commercial commission and noteworthy for its many innovations, such as a boxy redbrick fortresslike exterior; large, open interior spaces that collected light; stained glass windows; air-conditioning; built-in desk furniture; and toilet bowls suspended from the walls. Sadly, it was demolished in 1950, much to the dismay of preservationists.

Along Buffalo's Black Rock Channel you can tour Frank Lloyd Wright's Fontana Boathouse, while the Peace Bridge, with its five arched spans, shows off in the background. Buffalo's West Side Rowing Club, the nation's largest youth-based rowing club, runs a number of its programs out of the five-thousand-square-foot space. The two-story structure with red oak doors and trim and a cantilevered roof was originally designed in 1905 for a site at the University of Wisconsin but was never constructed. It's now called the Fontana Boathouse since Buffalo native and television writer/producer Tom Fontana (*Oz* and *St. Elsewhere*, among many others) helped raise $5.5 million from his Hollywood friends, including Mary Tyler Moore, Blythe Danner, and producer Diane English. Tom named it after his father, Charles, a renowned rowing coach, and his mother, Marie, but that's not on the building because "Take me to the Charles and Marie Fontana Boathouse" is too hard to say at five o'clock in the morning. Marie and my friend Pete lived in the same building for many years, and Marie was the office manager for my mom's doctor—more examples of why Buffalo continues to feel like Mayberry rather than a metropolis.

Along similar horizontal lines, a filling station constructed according to Wright's 1927 preliminary plans is currently in the works and will be housed inside an addition to the Buffalo Transportation Pierce-Arrow Museum. The two-story building with a cantilevered copper roof atop red and white concrete paving won't have any gas or gum for sale. And I'm not sure it will be completed anytime soon since currently you have to phone ahead to make sure the museum is open. But it's worth the call and the trip, not just to gawk at the marvelous old cars, but also to giggle at the crazy Snoopy and the Red Baron leather caps, goggles, silk scarves, and other outlandish getups people would don to go motoring. *What were they thinking?* one wonders, especially while boarding a plane alongside folks in citrus green tracksuits with appliquéd cats, bottomed off by sunflower yellow sheepskin Ugg boots or purple plastic Crocs dotted with Jibbitz flag, flower, and insect charms.

Several new best-selling bodice rippers have been revisiting Wright's bad-boy celebrity credentials as of late. After twenty years of marriage and six children, he scandalously left his spouse for a neighbor's wife (basically breaking commandments seven through ten in one swell foop). A few years later, a crazed servant set fire to the home they'd set up together, killing the woman and her two children along with four others. Wright married again, but his bride was addicted to morphine, so that didn't last long. Finally, he wedded Montenegrin dancer Olgivanna Ivanovna Lazovich, thirty years his junior, who inspired his work with her theosophical leanings—speculation about the workings of the soul based on mystical insight into the nature of God. She'd also been a pupil of the Greek Armenian mystic G. I.

Gurdjieff, promoter of the Fourth Way, which emphasized inner development through simultaneously strengthening the mind, body, and emotions. I suppose this is the place to mention that Wright was a Unitarian.

As a believer in the unity of all things, Wright strove to create architecture that was an expression of divinity and would engage in a dialogue with nature. The strong emphasis on horizontal lines and planes and hovering roofs suggests a belonging to the earth beneath them. And like Elbert Hubbard, he also became fond of an unmistakable "I'm an *artiste*" look, which involved long, flowing hair, a broad-brimmed hat, a swirling cape, a cravat, and a dramatic black cane not used for walking so much as to punctuate his sentences.

Wright's maternal grandfather, Richard Lloyd Jones (1799–1885), was a Unitarian minister from Wales who championed freedom of religion and political reform. The seventh of their ten children, Jenkin Lloyd Jones (1843–1918), also became a Unitarian minister, but eventually didn't want to be identified with any established religion and built a new church in Chicago called "All Souls, a people's church." He believed in harnessing a common effort to improve human life, moved away from Christian sermons toward educational and inspirational addresses, and invited guests of different creeds and nationalities to exchange pulpits with him. After Jones served as a private in the Civil War and fought in eleven battles including Vicksburg, he became a pacifist and preached that war solved nothing but was merely a tool used by politicians and businessmen to advance their own agendas, which could usually be reduced to profit and power. He was also an early advocate of equal rights and opportunities for women. Seriously, with all those crackpot ideas, no wonder so many people thought the man was touched.

Frank Lloyd Wright's father, William Wright, had been a Baptist minister, but he later joined his wife's family in the

Unitarian faith. Wright's older half brother, William, would follow their father into the ministry. Wright's cousin, Richard Lloyd Jones (1873–1963), was the outspoken owner and editor of the *Tulsa Tribune*, a founder of All Souls Unitarian Church in Tulsa, Oklahoma, and instrumental in creating the Abraham Lincoln Birthplace National Historic Site. However, his reputation is somewhat tarnished for having scribed an editorial that allegedly helped incite the 1921 Tulsa Race Riot against blacks.

Frank Lloyd Wright designed Unity Temple for the Unitarian congregation in Oak Park, Illinois, which is now considered by many to be the first modern building in the world, and also the innovative, landmark First Unitarian Society Meeting House in Madison, Wisconsin. Both have undergone extensive renovations.

Wright's best legacy of all, in my opinion, lies in his son John Lloyd Wright's invention of Lincoln Logs, so that kids everywhere could construct their own dream houses.

Good Bones

Frank Lloyd Wright couldn't be riding a bigger wave of popularity right now if he'd invented solar-heated homes, but his contribution makes up only a fraction of the superb local architecture. Though more commonly associated with machine shops and smokestacks, Buffalo is home to the world's earliest skyscrapers. The ten-story Ellicott Square Building, designed by Daniel Burnham, was the largest office building in the world for sixteen years after it opened in 1896. Built in the Italian Renaissance style, it contains a majestic interior courtyard and a marble mosaic floor depicting sun symbols from civilizations around the world. Louis Sullivan's thirteen-story Guaranty Building (now called the Prudential Building), completed in 1895, is another standout, with strong vertical lines and a heavily ornamented facade of elaborate terra-cotta designs. Buffalo's magnificent City Hall, completed in 1931, is considered a tour de force of civic architecture and one of the most striking art deco buildings in the country. Friezes, symbolic figures, and tile work tell the story of Buffalo, at least the good parts. The center of the high-domed lobby ceiling depicts the sun, a welcome sight in the middle of December.

Free tours of City Hall are available every day at noon. I say this for two reasons. Obviously, the first is that they're free, but the second is that the information booth seems to have fallen victim to a budget cut. Likewise, so has much of the lighting, thus be sure to bring a flashlight or wear a miner's hat if you want to appreciate all the phenomenal detail work. And the cooling system is dodgy at best, so dress accordingly.

The grand art deco–style Buffalo Central Terminal, with its famed seventeen-story clock tower, opened in 1929 and handled more than two hundred passenger trains a day. The planners showed great optimism by including a liquor store in the blueprints, even though it was the height of Prohibition. However, the train station began operating only weeks before the crash of 1929, and with the onset of the Great Depression, followed by a decline in rail travel, it was never able to fulfill its potential. The last train departed in 1979, and the building fell on hard times. As locals like to say about a number of municipal developments, it was the wrong project in the wrong place at the wrong time. Still, standing among the glorious ruins and gazing out at the weed-choked tracks, it's possible to imagine fedora-topped businessmen heading for Chicago, chinchilla-wrapped women on their way to New York, and soldiers shipping off to fight Herr Hitler, their tearful young brides on the platform, wondering if these young men would come back.

The terminal is undergoing a loving renovation, most of the work and fund-raising performed by volunteers. We're on Obama's list of cities to get a bullet train one of these decades, and the idea is that, like a phoenix rising from its own ashes, Central Terminal will make a miraculous comeback. In the meantime, the building is open for tours and special events, so long as you don't mind a draft and brownouts. And it's obvious that locals care about the building, not just because visitors currently have to use Porta Potties, but because for the first tour a few hundred people were expected and three thousand turned up!

If you're planning a visit to Buffalo, consider staying at the Mansion on Delaware Avenue, a Second Empire–style home built in 1869, with two curved flights of marble steps and cast-iron Corinthian columns, eighteen-foot ceilings, twenty-eight guest rooms, and enormous bay windows. It's been converted from a dilapidated eyesore to one of the finest hotels in the country. With butlers on call twenty-four hours and a gourmet continental breakfast, a stay here would cost five times as much in Manhattan, and you'd have horns honking outside night and day.

A master plan to reuse the Buffalo Psychiatric Center near Elmwood Avenue, which looms empty and abandoned over the city's West Side, is also currently under way. The only small stumbling block is that the city and state have no funds for such a project. Fortunately, none of this prevents locals from using the line "I'll call and tell the Psych Center you're coming."

This brown Medina sandstone and redbrick building complex is an architectural gem by Henry Hobson Richardson (1836–1886), who also designed the First Unitarian Universalist Church in Springfield, Massachusetts, and the Brattle Square Church in Boston, which was built for a Unitarian congregation but is now First Baptist Church.

Richardson was known for employing a heavy-looking Romanesque style of soaring towers flanked by squat brick pavilions, pointed Gothic arches, and basically anything else castlelike that makes you glance around for a drawbridge over a moat and crusaders trotting off to recover the Holy Land while picking up a couple of cities and a few gold trinkets along the way. Richardson is regarded as the first of the three greatest American architects, the other two being Louis Sullivan and Frank Lloyd Wright. The grounds of the Psych Center were designed by renowned landscape architect Frederick Law Olmsted, famous for Manhattan's Central Park and Buffalo's Delaware Park. When my mom was a kid in the 1940s, it was still called the very homey insane asylum. She and her brother and sister would attempt a shortcut across the grounds to get to the Rees Street public swimming pool, but the guards usually stopped them, although this may have been because they'd occasionally pick some fruit along the way. The central administration edifice plus five separate but connected buildings and expansive grounds were mostly self-supporting, with their own laundry, bakery, and gardens. My maternal grandmother worked there as an aide in the 1950s when it was called the Buffalo State Hospital, and my mother worked there as a psychiatric nurse in the 1980s after it had become the Buffalo Psych Center.

When it first opened in 1880, the Psych Center was considered state-of-the-art care for the mentally ill. It was built on the Kirkbride Plan, which allowed for maximum light and air in narrow buildings arranged so that the residents progressed toward the administrative center as they became ready for discharge. This didn't always go exactly according to plan, as evidenced by the fact that in the file of one of my mother's patients she found notes made by her own mother from forty years earlier.

Buffalo is also home to a number of impressive works of public art and outdoor monuments, including statues of Commodore Oliver Hazard Perry (Front Park), Millard Fillmore and former mayor and president Grover Cleveland (both outside City Hall), and an exact replica of Michelangelo's *David* (Delaware Park, looking out over the Scajaquada Expressway). It's hard to imagine what Michelangelo would have to say about people getting a three-second glimpse of his masterpiece while whizzing past at sixty miles per hour.

There's a statue of a young Abraham Lincoln sitting on an oak log with an ax at his feet and a book on his right knee, cleverly titled *Young Lincoln*, between Lincoln Parkway and Delaware Park's Rose Garden, and also a large bronze somewhat older Abe, *Lincoln the Emancipator*, at the back of the Buffalo and Erie County Historical Society, overlooking Hoyt Lake.

Mathematically speaking, for each time he passed through Buffalo, Lincoln ended up with a statue. The first visit was on the way to his inauguration in February of 1861.

Buffalonians had voted for Lincoln, but not by a large margin. Still, most people dropped what they were doing and rushed to Exchange Street Station to catch sight of the president-elect. "Women fainted, men were crushed under the mass of bodies and many others had their bones broken. Once out of the depot every man uttered a brief 'Thank God!' for the preservation of his life. More with personal injuries were carried away and the fainted women were recovering under a free use of hydrant water," according to the Buffalo *Commercial Advertiser*. Mr. and Mrs. Lincoln hosted a reception at the American Hotel and the following day attended service at the Unitarian church with Millard Fillmore and his wife.

The second visit was under very different circumstances, following Lincoln's assassination five days after the Civil War ended. His westward funeral procession stopped in Buffalo on April 27, 1865, where the president lay in state in Saint James Hall at Washington and Eagle streets.

Living Here in Allentown

No, not that one. Our Allentown is a neighborhood just north of the heart of downtown Buffalo known for its antique stores, galleries, clothing boutiques, restaurants, and "angelheaded hipsters burning for the ancient heavenly connection," as Allen Ginsberg so aptly put it in *Howl*. "What's shaking, Daddy-O?" may have segued into "Whassup, Dude?" but it's still where one goes to sip coffee while discussing the influence of German Romanticism on postcolonial theory.

Now a historic preservation district, the area has been host for more than fifty years to an art festival the second weekend of every June that should not be missed—and isn't by most Buffalonians, based on the throngs that turn out. They come in cars, on buses, bicycles, scooters, and motorcycles, pulling wagons, and pushing strollers with cup holders. There are so many wheelchairs, canes, and crutches that you might accidentally think a Lourdes satellite shrine was offering a special on healing. More than a few long-haired, sandal-clad festival wanderers bear a passing resemblance to Jesus, so those awaiting the return of the Messiah may have to devise a questionnaire.

Over four hundred artists from around the country exhibit their pottery, metal sculpture, jewelry, furniture, blown glass, birdhouses, wooden toys, fountains, embroidery, handcrafted cutting boards, and oil paintings that you'd be proud to hang in your living room. There are stained glass flip-flops, black soap, hemp T-shirts, magic towel holders, and framed photos of puffins in every position imaginable but still suitable for a family audience. People in this country must be positively hoarding wind chimes based on the vast supply and selection.

The culinary fare is probably not for those who thrive close to the bottom of the food chain or think that *Food, Inc.* was the best documentary film of 2009. Long lines form in front of stalls selling Philly cheesesteak, roast beef on weck, Italian sausage, pizza, curly fries, fried dough, Italian pastry, deep-fried Twinkies and Oreos, onion rings, and funnel cake. The most outrageous offering is at a stand carrying not only barbecued wild boar, but alligator po'boys. When asked if it's real alligator, as many festivalgoers do, a server points to the six-foot gator roasting on a spit over on the sidewalk.

Exhibitors sell their homemade bread-and-butter pickles, pickled beets, and soy candles (eat or burn?). Catering to the locals, an artist offers carved wooden and metal Buffalo napkin caddies, key holders, welcome signs, and coatracks. There's an abundance of tie-dyed, beaded, and flowing clothing that will guarantee that you can pass as a folksinger. Booths offer henna body art to brighten up pale Buffalo skin and chess lessons for the high-minded.

But the real appeal of the Allentown Art Festival is the bohemian bonhomie. People run into friends and stand around talking and laughing for hours. Casually dressed locals stroll past stalls accompanied by bandanna-wearing mutts. Buskers send out swirls of jazzy riffs on saxes and clarinets and then pass the hat. Artsy types create mythical scenes with sidewalk chalk. Performers take their acts into the street, costumed as knights, reciting poetry, and dancing to boom boxes or just the music playing in their own minds. Enterprising neighborhood residents find it an ideal time for weekend porch parties and tag sales. A few cops mill about drinking cups of joe, also running into friends and having a grand old time while keeping Allentown safe for yakety yakking, Mohammedan angels, and hydrogen jukeboxes.

The rest of the year I head to Allentown to enjoy all kinds of great food, from The Towne restaurant's famed spanakopita and Cozumel's stuffed mushrooms to Quaker Bonnet's elephant ears (crispy, sweet cinnamon Danish) and the Rue Franklin's warm raspberry gratin, and to walk among a mixture of fine and funky architecture. The Secrets of Allentown tour, held in early fall, will gain you entrée into some spectacular private residences. However, the recently renovated Wilcox Mansion, where Theodore Roosevelt was inaugurated in 1901, following the assassination of William McKinley, is open daily to the public and offers tours on the half hour. The twenty-sixth president didn't stay long in Buffalo, but I think this American original and foremost urban cowboy, who actually had to borrow a proper suit, coat, and shoes for the swearing-in ceremony, would have felt right at home living here in Allentown.

Buffalo Past and Prologue

It's a shame the entire Western New York workforce didn't triumph the way local working girls did at the start of the 1901 Pan-Am Exposition. When out-of-town prostitutes invaded their turf, what followed was eight hours of scratching, biting, and hair pulling that police classified as a full-scale riot. The interlopers were ordered to leave, and a Buffalo newspaper reporter described it as a "noteworthy victory for hometown industry."

The Rust Belt blues is an oft-sung and well-known tune by now. Heavy industry and manufacturing moved south and overseas, taking half the population along with it. Grain transportation, which had once been the lifeblood of Buffalo, bypassed the city following the opening of the Saint Lawrence Seaway, in 1959.

Meantime, the advent of electric refrigeration put an end to the harvest and shipment of ice throughout the Northeast, and as far away as Cuba and the West Indies. The subterranean springs that fed several lakes southeast of the city, Cattaraugus County's Lime Lake in particular, created marvelous crops of clean ice that could be used in cooking and refreshments. At its peak in the late 1800s and early 1900s, the industry harvested and sold over 150,000 tons of ice while providing jobs for six hundred men per season and almost as many horses. One clever quadruped soon caught on to the fact that if he fell into the water he received a shot of moonshine to warm up, and thus he began diving into the drink whenever he felt like a quick pick-me-up. I suspect that when the ice age dried up, this enterprising horse hoofed it to Atlantic City and took up high diving off the famous Steel Pier.

Mark Twain, who famously exhorted, "Cold! If the thermometer had been an inch longer, we'd have all frozen to death," took a one-third interest in and was coeditor of the *Buffalo Express* (which would merge with the *Buffalo Courier* in 1926 and go out of business in 1982), but left in 1871, after less than two years. Our city somehow became a stopping point rather than a staying place for a number of people on their way to better things. American writer F. Scott Fitzgerald, who epitomized the Jazz Age, spent the years 1898 to 1901 and 1903 to 1908 in Buffalo, where he attended Holy Angels and then Nardin Academy while his father worked as a soap salesman for Procter & Gamble. When Fitzgerald was almost twelve, his father lost that job and the family returned to Saint Paul, Minnesota. Most people think his short stories were inspired by Saint Paul and take place there, but we know better. Fitzgerald cleverly disguised his work so as not to have statues erected and parks and theaters named for him all over Buffalo.

The 1980s gave rise to a local organization called Buffalonians by Choice as a way of distinguishing between those freely opting to reside in the area and those being held against their will in hostage/captive situations. Similar optimism-turned-desperation produced a T-shirt that reads Buffalo—Looking Better Every Day. This goes nicely with the existential moniker coined by local artist Michael Morgulis, City of No Illusions. That's right. We don't walk around acting as if we're Pittsburgh or Milwaukee.

Since the decline of Big Steel and auto manufacturing, Buffalo has been working on nurturing replacement industries to satisfy the New World Order. Medical research and development has burgeoned in the areas of human genome research and bioinformatics (the application of information technology to the field of molecular biology), led by the University at Buffalo and the world-renowned Roswell Park Cancer Institute.

The area is now said to be the hub of a "golden horseshoe" containing 650 biomedical firms within less than a ninety-minute drive, a veritable Lake District, but with an emphasis on cell replication as opposed to romantic poetry.

Buffalo serves as the headquarters of M&T Bank and First Niagara Financial Group, along with being home to major operations of other financial institutions such as HSBC Bank USA and KeyBank. It's the headquarters for Merchants Insurance Group; Rich Products, one of the largest privately owned companies in the country; global food service and hospitality provider Delaware North Companies; and Labatt moved its US home office there in 2007. Sports licensing headwear company New Era Cap, the exclusive manufacturer of the official on-field caps worn by every Major League Baseball team and their minor-league affiliates, has taken over the former Federal Reserve Building (with a government deficit like this, who needs a bank?).

M&T Bank is a great corporate citizen, and you'll see their name on everything from the rain forest at the zoo to the refurbished clock in Central Terminal, along with being listed as a donor, sponsor, or underwriter of numerous sporting events and cultural activities. "The city went through a tough time, but we have great people, arts, architecture, restaurants, sports teams, and a wonderful zoo," said Bob Wilmers, M&T Bank's chairman and CEO. "It's my city and I want to see it be one of the best in the United States."

Can any or all of this work? In 1972, when Chinese politician Zhou Enlai was asked about the impact of the French Revolution of 1789 he replied, "It's too early to tell."

There are problems, just like anywhere else, especially those that go hand in hand with high rates of poverty and unemployment. While 80 percent of African American workers live in the city, many new jobs are in the suburbs, and sufficient public transportation isn't available. Currently, there are plans under way or on the drawing board to improve education and literacy, provide more job training and summer youth jobs, and deal with derelict housing.

The Buffalo schools are hit-or-miss. Some, like City Honors, regularly make the lists of top schools in the nation, along with Tapestry Charter (K–12), famous for its low teacher/student ratio and heavy parent involvement. International students, mostly from Asia, are increasingly enrolling at local private schools Nichols, Buffalo Seminary, and The Park School. On the opposite end, there are closures and failures. City schools are burdened with massive legacy costs from aging infrastructure, a declining tax base, rampant bureaucracy, and the problems attendant upon indigent families. Meantime, the high rate of teen pregnancy and STDs would suggest that an Unplanned Parenthood is operating in the area.

More than two dozen colleges and universities provide an excellent source of growth, according to urban activist and social entrepreneur Newell Nussbaumer, since they bring in ten thousand new students a year, some of whom will decide to stay. Also known as the unofficial mayor of Buffalo for all of his creative boosterism, Nussbaumer started the website www.navigetter.com as a resource to learn what's going on locally. It includes bike trails, meeting places, events, shopping, activities for a cold day, and community gardens and other projects you can work on.

The Albright-Knox Art Gallery, with its world-renowned collection of modern and contemporary art, has been delighting locals and visitors since 1905. In fact, the US Postal Service recently released a new series of ten stamps based on the abstract expressionist movement, and four of them feature artwork from this famed Buffalo gallery.

In 2008, the Burchfield Penney Art Center moved to a new home on fashion-forward Elmwood Avenue. This sleek zinc and stone museum is dedicated to displaying local artists and contains over a hundred works of watercolorist Charles Burchfield (1893–1967), who spent all but the first few years of his career in the Buffalo area. With Burchfield's moody, probing, and often phantasmagorical style, it couldn't be more appropriate that the museum is located right next to the imposing Scooby-Doo-spooky Psych Center. And the nearby Grecian templelike Buffalo and Erie County Historical Society Museum mounts some terrific shows, including one for the Buffalo Bills' recent fiftieth anniversary, but perhaps it's better known as the place locals go to research the details of their history-filled homes and ascertain what ghosts to expect.

Buffalo-area book lovers are well served by chain stores Barnes & Noble and Borders; indies Talking Leaves and Book Corner; and secondhand shops such as Queen City, Rustbelt Books, Oracle Junction, Second Reader, and Old Editions. Furthermore, the most complete collection of James Joyce manuscripts and memorabilia is housed at the University at Buffalo. It includes writer's notebooks, letters, and fantastic photographs, thereby making the area a natural to host Joyce conferences, exhibits, and an estimable Bloomsday celebration. Why all this Eire on Erie? one might well ask. Well, um, for starters the words *Buffalo* and *Ireland* both contain seven letters.

The outdoor Allentown Arts Festival in July and Taste of Buffalo a few weeks later both attract half a million people. Meantime, there's no need to go to Conor McPherson's *The Seafarer* on Broadway when, with more than twenty area theater companies, an excellent production is available at the New Phoenix Theatre on the Park in downtown Buffalo. Same with *The Farnsworth Invention* at the Kavinoky Theatre. Our very own Nickel City Opera offers high-class productions at the historic Riviera Theatre in North Tonawanda,

home of the Mighty Wurlitzer Organ. And simulcasts from
the Metropolitan Opera beamed live into local movie theaters play to packed houses. The good news is that the price
is one-tenth what a Met ticket would cost, and you can't get
Jujubes at Lincoln Center. The bad news is that cell phones
go off and there's a line for the ladies room during intermis-
sion in both places. In addition to plenty of movie theaters,
there are also several film festivals that draw thousands of
participants.

Buffalo has always been home to a thriving music scene,
and many people believe the city held a legitimate claim to
the Rock and Roll Hall of Fame, which eventually wound
up in Cleveland. We can thank the early Canal District,
where sailors, saloonkeepers, and ladies of the night with
names like Pug Nose Cora and Deadly Dora were in need
of a soundtrack for their métier prior to the advent of radios
and record players. In fact, the minstrel show—variety acts,
songs, and dance performed by white performers in black-
face—is thought to have originated in 1839 with a performance by Edwin P. Christy in Mrs. Harrington's dance hall.
This popular entertainment grew into Christy's Minstrels,
featuring their big hit song "Buffalo Gals," and moved to the
more respectable Eagle Street Theater outside of the red-light
district. From there, it was off to a long run on Broadway.

As the population grew and the economy flourished,
so did the number of ballrooms, gin mills, and dance halls.
African Americans had their own prosperous combos, singers, clubs, and local union up through the 1960s. In Buffalo's melting pot, many different cultures combined their
musical traditions and lots of Jewish kids were forced into
lessons at an early age. Before people aspired to be sports
stars, supermodels, reality show contestants, and TV judges,
they dreamed of being musicians. With so many bars and
churches, there were always plenty of places for garage bands

and fledgling groups to find their groove. Then there's the stellar Buffalo Philharmonic Orchestra, which named JoAnn Falletta its music director in 1999, the first female to hold this post in its seventy-five-year history. The orchestra has won two Grammy awards and can be heard on the soundtrack of Woody Allen's film *Manhattan*. Performances take place in the neoclassically radiant Kleinhans Music Hall, a national historic landmark designed by Eliel and Eero Saarinen and considered to be one of the finest concert halls in the country.

In addition to oodles of Bach, blues, brass, head-banging rock, indie pop, and hip-hop, one can just as easily find polka, barbershop quartets, square dancing, a cappella, karaoke, and the chicken dance (mostly at weddings). Reminiscent of its days as a key stop for vaudeville (George Burns, Gracie Allen, and Gypsy Rose Lee), performers on the Chitlin Circuit (Aretha Franklin, Ray Charles, and Wilson Pickett), and the big bands of the 1940s, Buffalo continues to play host to world-renown musical talent, such as the Grateful Dead, U2, Bruce Springsteen, Janet Jackson, Garth Brooks, and most touring Broadway shows. Homegrown Grammy Award–winning Ani DiFranco and her manager Scot Fisher recently saved the nineteenth-century Gothic Revival–style Asbury Delaware Methodist Church from the wrecking ball and converted it into a light and spacious center to worship the visual and performing arts, rechristening it "Babeville," after their Righteous Babe recording label.

Plenty of live music can be heard in Buffalo's hottest club-hopping neighborhoods—rowdy Chippewa Street; the hipster- and alternative-lifestyle-encompassing Allentown; Elmwood Village, which attracts a mix of young and old; and the college-crowd hangouts on Main Street that are within walking distance of UB's south campus. Disc jockeys presiding over dance parties of electro, techno, trance, and hypertempo can be found throughout Buffalo and are so popular that exciting DJs come from around the country to guest host. Upcoming gigs and reviews are listed in *The Buffalo News*'s "Gusto" section and the weekly *Artvoice*, which also offers intelligent commentary on local business and politics.

You can't enjoy good music without good beer, and Buffalo has never been known to let anyone go thirsty. In addition to the many and various gin mills, local breweries such as Pearl Street Grill & Brewery and Flying Bison Brewing Company keep quality libations flowing. The popular Buffalo Brewfest is a beer-tasting festival that brings hops connoisseurs together every August while raising money for local charities. Designated drivers are admitted for free. (Fortunately, the Buffalo Chili Fest is several months beforehand, in April, since it might not be wise, gastrointestinally speaking, to attend both on the same weekend.)

Every year on the Saturday after Thanksgiving, the World's Largest Disco, a tribute to the 1970s, attracts not only thousands of partygoers to the Buffalo Convention Center, but half the cast of *The Brady Bunch*. Tickets to this charity fund-raiser sell out in minutes, so don't expect to make it to the box office in time wearing high-heeled sneakers or rainbow wedges. Why Buffalo and disco? Maybe because local Litelab Corporation produced the lighted dance floor seen in *Saturday Night Fever*. Then again, maybe not.

The Colored Musicians Club in the Michigan Street African American Heritage Corridor is opening a museum to celebrate being the longest continuously operating colored musicians club in the country and the only remaining African American music club in the United States. It was formed in 1918 by members of the Colored Musicians Union, which had been started a year earlier by black musicians denied membership in the white musicians' local. Despite having (just barely) survived the seventies, the Colored Musicians Club is all about jazz and big band, so please don't show up in a unitard and expect to do the hustle. Or to see any stars from *The Partridge Family*.

All the big-name comedians come through town, including Jerry Seinfeld, Paula Poundstone, Lewis Black, Jeff Foxworthy, Chelsea Handler, and Katt Williams. We may not have good body surfing on Lake Erie, but Buffalonians know how to laugh and tell jokes. How could we not have a sense of humor with area funeral homes named Amigone (add your own question mark) and Bury? And with runners in the annual Turkey Trot, one of the oldest road races in America, dressing as actual turkeys among a crowded field of centipedes, superheroes, and flamingos. Some singing. A few on stilts.

As a kid, I remember most of my teachers and neighbors and especially the local shopkeepers as being funny. Today I find the same sort of casual jokiness that makes life more pleasant during daily transactions with almost everyone I meet, except for the immigration officers at the Peace Bridge, who go so far as to put out signs warning that they possess NO sense of humor. The families of my Jewish godparents hailed from *Fiddler on the Roof* Russia and war-torn Europe. For this reason, my godfather, Irving, wouldn't allow any German music played in the house, German art on the walls, or German cars in the driveway. He loved auctions and once purchased a lot that contained a painting by a Teutonic landscape artist that quickly ended up in our living room. I used to wish he'd accidently purchase a Mercedes-Benz that would land in our driveway to replace our Detroit lemons, which started on alternate days of the week. Whenever something small went wrong, like when Irving's electric car window wouldn't go down or when his plastic fork snapped, he was fond of saying, "First Hitler, now this!" That was my introduction to Yiddish humor.

To up the local fun quotient, if that's possible, boating and ice-skating have returned to Delaware Park, a pastoral oasis in the middle of the city with 350 acres of meadow, forest, and lake. At least it's tranquil, aside from the Golf War—a spirited debate over whether the park should or should not boast an eighteen-hole golf course, which it currently does. Since 1976, the park has also been host to a popular *free* Shakespeare festival. On a glorious summer night, behind the rose garden, it's possible to hear Hamlet exclaim from a Tudor-style stage beneath a sky quilted with stars, "The play's the thing!" while chirruping crickets provide the chorus. On the flip side, occasionally an actual tempest interrupts *The Tempest*.

Despite all this activity, there are rarely any traffic jams in Buffalo, even during rush hour, when you can still rush from one place to another in a matter of minutes, or to a Bills game. In fact, rush hour usually means exactly that: people driving faster because they need to get to work or want to go home. And best of all, the bars stay open late in order to cut down on drunk driving.

The new Squaw Island Park is located in the Black Rock section of Buffalo and accessible by railroad swing bridge. This converted landfill is now ready for fishing, bird-watching, walking, biking, and picnicking. It's largely hidden and still somewhat undiscovered.

An hour southwest of Buffalo, on the tranquil shores of Cassadaga Lake, sits the spiritual community of Lily Dale. This psychic center is a great conversation starter in Western New York since almost everyone has a Lily Dale story. And if you tell people you're going, they'll most certainly inquire if you have "the gift," which means that they do and be sure to ask them about it.

Bring directions. My GPS doesn't register Lily Dale and I had to assume it was removed for the same reason Dick

Cheney's bunker is blacked out. Once safely there, you can enjoy private readings or join the daily message service at Inspiration Stump, an energy vortex that assists in connecting to the astral plane. The last time I visited, the spirits sent a message via hailstorm saying that the meeting should be moved inside of Assembly Hall. Several mediums conduct a this world/next world call-and-response, in which they describe to the entire group a person on the other side who is sending a communiqué and audience members can then identify themselves as the recipients. One thing I noticed is that the messages usually come from someone named Mary, Richard, or Jeff and rarely a Hortense, Jasper, or Ignatius. Similarly, the person who has crossed over tended to like jazz or rock or Frank Sinatra rather than marimba bands or panpipes or Panic! At The Disco. And the ailments they suffered from most often were heart trouble or cancer-related as opposed to Fuchs' corneal dystrophy, rectal fissures, or a flesh-eating virus. I was rather hoping that one of the mediums would point at someone and say, "I can read your mind, and you should be ashamed of yourself," but none of them did. Still, whether you have "the gift" or not, are a believer or not, are there in body or just in spirit, it makes for a fun day.

A half hour from Lily Dale is the Chautauqua Institution, perched on the northwestern edge of scenic Chautauqua Lake, an old Seneca word for either "bag tied in the middle," as this describes the shape of the lake, or else "wear batik clothing and carry a quilted shoulder bag," as this describes most of the clientele. Either way, lifelong learners have been coming from around the country to the Chautauqua Institution to enlarge, enlighten, and ennoble themselves with educational programs and entertainment for more than 135 years. Presenters include everyone from presidents, journalists, and professors to pop stars, big bands, and orchestras. There are even rumors that one of the cozy gingerbread cottages serves as headquarters for a top secret UU Mafia that goes around in shiny hemp suits and unisex Bass penny Weejuns fighting reverse reverse discrimination. So if you're in the Unitarian Witness Protection Program (or just have an aversion to white wicker furniture), this is not a good place to vacation, particularly in the vicinity of any mystic heart learning circles or gourd pottery classes. In fact, although it's probably against the rules, I know a lot of UUs who want their ashes scattered behind the Hall of Philosophy, where many happy hours were spent in talkbacks about social witnessing, peacemongering, ethical eating, and bee colony collapse, all accompanied by faint whispers of an international Unitarian conspiracy that has been credited with permanently grounding the super environmentally unfriendly Concorde supersonic airliner.

Drive across the Peace Bridge from the West Side of Buffalo to historic Fort Erie, Canada, and save yourself a time-machine trip to ancient Greece by visiting the classically designed Point Abino Lighthouse. It's inside a private community, but if you're nice and don't have any visible explosives strapped to your chest, they'll let you look. Then drop by the Bridgeburg secondhand bookstore on Jarvis Street, neatly tucked in among the pawnshop and tattoo parlor. Try and arrive around noon so as to catch the Chipwagon, a.k.a. the French fry truck. Bridgeburg Bookstore's warm and welcoming sole proprietor, Annie, will be glad to tell you her name really is Annie Hall and isn't that ridiculous, and how her husband ran off with a twenty-year-old, but she bears him no ill will because people fall in love and what can you do, and that she probably drinks too much wine, and sleeps in bed with thirty or so books surrounding her, and will get on the Internet one of these days, along with taking her ex-husband's name off the sign and organizing the downstairs. Many of Annie's best volumes are stored in the mazelike basement, but she won't allow you to browse there because it's rather unorganized. That said, Pete managed to talk his way down in about ten minutes, so I guess the challenge is there for true bibliophiles. The best lav, according to my source on this subject, is at Coffee Culture, three doors down.

Next, drive ten minutes through some spectacular wine country to Niagara-on-the-Lake and see a brilliant revival of *The Little Foxes* or *Born Yesterday* at the Shaw Festival. Crowds are manageable, staff is friendly, and there's rarely a line to use the well-maintained women's restrooms.

As if good lavatories aren't reason enough to drop everything and plan a trip, *The New York Times* recently named Buffalo one of forty-four places in the world to visit, comfortably nestled among hot spots such as Phuket, Bhutan, Cuba, Hawaii, and Zambia. Ironically, the report landed on frigid front porches during a monthlong Arctic blast known as an Alberta clipper, a mass of cold air that rushes into the region from the north and is Canadian for "butt-freezing cold."

City of Great Neighbors (and Cat People)

Yes, you'll find upstanding citizens and good-hearted people everywhere, just like you'll find sociopaths and tail-pullers. But I do believe Buffalo's designation as the City of Good Neighbors, where a true friend lends you his last pair of long johns, is not only earned but deserved. The examples go on forever, and include residents returned to their homes in eleven days and not the six weeks federal agents said it might take after the Clarence plane crash, the well-documented community assistance and generosity shown to victims of disaster, such as the Amherst family left homeless by a mud slide and the Kenmore clan who lost their home and family dog in a Christmas Eve blaze. Now add to this countless unrecorded acts of humanity performed on a daily basis for friends and strangers alike. When *Extreme Makeover: Home Edition* shot an episode in Buffalo, over four thousand volunteers turned out, including many local craftsmen. It was the largest number of volunteers the TV show had ever seen and more than triple the number they typically attract in other places around the country.

One trait in particular I feel necessary to highlight is that when a butcher in Western New York calls out, "Who's next?" five people don't yell out their order as is the case in Me-First Manhattan, where "Excuse me!" serves as a direct threat rather than a polite request or an apology. Similarly, the height-challenged don't stealthily move to the front of a waiting crowd as if they're just trying to see into the display case when they're in fact strategically positioning themselves to catch the eye of the next available counterperson. No siree, when the "next" call goes out at Wegmans supermarket, people look around to see who is NEXT. Meantime, the old or infirm will almost always be ushered ahead, in case they're in a hurry to get to a lav. The employees at Wegmans are also terrifically pleasant and when asked for help, instead of proffering one of those vague sweeping arm gestures, will actually take you directly to the item you're in search of. The staff also has a fine sense of humor, as evidenced by of an employee who liked to glue silver dollars to the floor in front of the beer coolers on Saturday nights. The family-owned supermarket ranked third on *Fortune* magazine's 2010 list of 100 Best Places to Work and had been in the top ten for the eight years prior.

Similarly, it's with dignity that people shovel their driveways and mow their lawns along with the yards of their older relatives. Yes, some folks hire a service, but none would brag about it, well aware that personally attending to these tasks is a badge of honor rather than something to be looked down upon as a form of labor beneath them, including those with good jobs and more degrees than a thermometer. Just the opposite: shoveling is often hailed as the secret to longevity, after sponge candy. Stories about plucky old people almost always contain a line about how they were still out clearing the walk at age ninety-two. "I finally said, 'Grandpa, at least wait until it stops snowing so you don't have to go right back out and do it again.' But he wouldn't listen. And the Bills were playing the Patriots at one o'clock." In fact, some people take such pride in their snow-removal skills that upon finishing the clearing-out part they use the shovel to go around and *edge* their masterpiece.

Meantime, if you're wandering around a parking lot in Buffalo helplessly clicking your key with the hope that your vehicle will call out to you, rest assured that not one but several perfect strangers will offer to drive you around in search of your car. I know from experience. Rotarians are particularly dependable for this activity, and they're talented at locating my make and model.

By US standards, Western New York has been settled for a long time. Before police stations were organized, fire brigades were formed, hospitals were built, phone lines erected, and snowplows roared through the streets at dawn, people had to look out for one another and form networks of protection. And even as local services evolved, if you were an immigrant, a minority, or from the lower ranks of society, they weren't necessarily there to ensure *your* safety and well-being.

The area is steeped in agrarian roots, and if your barn was on fire or the family had typhus, it was the nearest neighbors who determined whether or not you survived. Thus, it wasn't a good idea to do anything to tick off said neighbors, even if you didn't like their politics or religion or music all that much. Nor was it a good idea to hold a grudge because their dog made peeing on your pachysandra appear to be a job that he was getting paid to perform.

My South African–born husband is astounded that people in the Midwest walk into each other's homes uninvited. What does he think the word *yoo-hoo* was invented for? Certainly not just to be the name of a beverage. Furthermore, as most Buffalo bedrooms contain an electric blanket, one rarely risks interrupting couples having sex on the kitchen table, even with their socks on.

Winters are protracted, or as Samuel Johnson said about *Paradise Lost*, "None ever wished it longer," and deadly storms on the eastern end of Lake Erie hit hard and fast. We are all too well aware that Mother Nature has stacked the deck, and she's no one to fool with if you value Father Time. Car trunks contain a shovel and a blanket. A Buffalonian's last words are rarely, "Hey, y'all, watch this!" except perhaps in the ice-fishing community.

If you're caught on the wrong side of a storm and need assistance, it's just as likely you'll be dependent on an ordinary citizen as a platoon of rescue workers. Similarly, a stranger in trouble may knock on your front door or car window. It's for this reason that if you call and wake Buffalonians in the middle of the night, they insist that they weren't sleeping, because you're probably stuck somewhere and they have to come and get you and don't want it to appear to be an inconvenience. Remember how you decided who to be friends with as a kid based on pool ownership? Well, this is the criterion for making adult friends (assuming you don't have a large Italian family)—who will come fetch you in a storm?

Bowling remains a popular sport in Buffalo because you stay put while the ball automatically comes back to you, without anyone having to chase after it. Throughout its history, Buffalo has never been a transient town. Families tend to stay in the area for generations. Residents sit out on sprawling front porches. In fact, few cities have porches this size or as many of them. Neighbors know what you're up to and with whom. Big Brother is watching via the earliest known social networking site—good old-fashioned gossip, making the world a smaller place since 500,000 BC.

It's been said that Buffalo isn't a small city or even a small town (because of its famous one degree of separation) but merely a large living room. Even the paper, *The Buffalo News*, despite its coverage of world and national events, feels more like a village chronicle by including an appeal to the Lancaster High School Class of 1965 for volunteers to help celebrate their forty-fifth reunion, a save-the-date for the South Buffalo American Legion chicken barbecue, tips for family fun, a report on a lawn tractor stolen from a garage, a long list of birthdays, and plenty of space for locals to chime in with a point of view about what's going on at home, across the nation, or around the world. There are problems and solutions—when cinnamon toothpaste irritates (get a prescription for medicated Magic Mouthwash), excessive dog scratching (apply Listerine, mineral oil, and water in equal parts to doggy hot spots)—and a spirited debate as to whether a basement or first-floor laundry is best. If your tastes run more to the racy and ribald, you'll need to turn to the *Amherst Bee* police blotter, which diligently tracks the nefarious doings of scheming squirrels, marauding raccoons, attacks by psychotic deer, naked people sprinting through backyards, geese tapping on library windows, lawn ornament decapitations and disappearances, and even the occasional shirt caught in a blender. Criminals, take warning: Western New York is a place where police still capture evildoers by tracking their footprints through the snow.

When I sat down to speak with Charity Vogel, daughter of *Buffalo News* reporter Mike Vogel, it turned out her father once worked with my uncle Jim "Never bring a knife to a gunfight" Watson at the *Buffalo Courier-Express*. When I was ten years old, I'd waved the two men off at the Erie Basin Marina as they set sail on a training exercise aboard the Norwegian tall ship *Christian Radich*. In other words, Google Earth isn't watching Buffalo-area residents so much as everyone they know from work, church/temple/mosque/synagogue, school, sports, and the crybaby matinee. Trips to the mall or stops at gas stations almost always involve running into acquaintances. Therefore, do not perform smash-and-grab robberies, leave the scene of an accident, or think that nude sunbathing, cross-dressing, or a karaoke addiction can be kept on the down low. Your parents and/or children will know about it in the time it takes to say the rosary. And definitely don't have an affair in Buffalo. My sources tell me that one needs to go at least twenty miles out of town. But Baltimore is even safer. There's a saying about small towns that just as easily applies to Buffalo: if you don't want anyone to know about it, then don't do it.

It's not easy for cats and dogs without homes or care-takers to survive our *Wuthering Heights* winters. The stray pooches that once populated the area are largely gone, having been taken in, joined the wild packs roaming Detroit, or else traded their fur coats for Ray-Bans and a life in the Sarasota sunshine. However, there are an estimated 100,000 feral felines, and that's where the cat ladies come in. Unfortunately, *cat lady* is often used in the pejorative, as in "crazy old cat lady," possibly because it sounds like "bag lady." But it shouldn't be, and they live among us as teachers, toll collectors, nurses, carpenters, and Scrabble champions. In fact, many have master's degrees, doctorates, and prettily appointed homes—granted, with lots of cat bric-a-brac. A small percentage of men even fall into this regal cat-caring category. They, like the cat ladies, work tirelessly to fix and feed strays living outdoors year-round, rescue their kittens, get them veterinary care, and place them in good homes.

For me, the true nobility of the cat lady is in her willingness to care for Persians and Himalayans, felines with hippie-length hair and lots of it. By all appearances it seems their only occupations are to eat, sleep, shed, and poop themselves. I'm just thinking that you may as well help out around a kitty hospice.

It's easily possible to fill every day volunteering at the SPCA, local shelters, and clinics, and attending the Ten Lives Club FurBall, Feral Cat Focus Dinner, ABC (Animal Birth Control) luncheon, and the City Kitty fund-raiser, and many good-hearted folks do exactly that. Meantime, Operation PETS accepts strays twice a month on Freaky Feral Fridays for spaying and neutering.

Most of the benefits are held in February and March, right before kitten season, when everyone would otherwise be too busy with hands-on rescue work. My favorite event is where the cats actually climb up to Jesus in "suffer the little children to come unto me" fashion, but on all fours. It was at this particular silent auction where, between a three-story cat condo and twin hemp scratching posts, I was surprised to find a gift basket filled with analgesics and cough suppressants. Did they know I was coming?

My aunt had twelve cats at one point. She wasn't supposed to shelter that many felines in her apartment, so when the landlord came by she traded on the fact that they all looked alike, and so long as they stayed about four in a room with a few under the beds, she could get away with saying she had only five. Something similar happened in my friend Julie's Italian Catholic family. Her grandmother had twelve children, which was not all that unusual for Buffalo back in the day, but they lived on a street with German families and didn't want to appear déclassé, so only four kids were allowed out to play at a time, also under the assumption that by looking fairly alike and moving around quickly they couldn't be told apart all that well.

Along with my former Sweet Home teacher Kathy LeFauve, my aunt Sue is now busy almost full-time with cat rescue work, and so she no longer raises the exotic-looking sable-colored, golden-eyed Burmese. I have to admit that I miss going to cat shows with her, where as a kid it was my job to bring Bloody Marys around to the judges all morning. Analyzing cat coats and features was obviously incredibly stressful work. But nowadays Aunt Sue always has a houseful of adorable foster kittens waiting for good homes. A retired English teacher, she writes up their Purrsonality Profiles in brilliantly creative and impressionistic prose, which has resulted in a 100 percent adoption rate. Most begin with "Perfect Pussycat Companion...," as I understand that the word *pet* can sound a controversial note in cat circles.

"Those who say that we are in a time when there are no heroes just don't know where to look," Ronald Reagan declared in his first inaugural address. He went on to say that they can be found among farmers and factory workers and people on both sides of the counter. "They are individuals and families whose taxes support the government and whose voluntary gifts support church, charity, culture, art, and education." And cat shelters, I might add.

Aside from its several nicknames such as Queen City, Nickel City, and City of Light, Buffalo is not known by any catchphrases the way Beirut was the Paris of the East and Nashville was the Athens of the South. Buffalo is not called Gateway to Eden, New York—Home of the Original Kazoo Company Factory, Museum, and Boutique Gift Shop, even though it is! Or else as the first stop on the road to nearby LeRoy, New York, the birthplace of Jell-O! Likewise, one doesn't often hear Saint Moritz called the Buffalo of the Swiss Alps, or Aspen, Colorado, referred to as the Buffalo of the West.

That said, although there are cities named Buffalo in many other states—Illinois, Indiana, Iowa, Minnesota, Missouri, North Dakota, Oklahoma, South Carolina, South Dakota, Texas, West Virginia, Wyoming, and two in Wisconsin—when a national newspaper or magazine refers to Buffalo, they almost always mean Buffalo, New York, home of God's Frozen People.

Despite the fact that the weather is cold for a good part of the year, Buffalonians are a warm, generous, high-spirited, and neighborly people, proud and protective of their turf. This is easily visible at any home game of the Buffalo Sabres, Bills, or Bisons, and something my husband experienced firsthand a few years back. As I mentioned, my husband was born and raised in South Africa, though his ancestors were Dutch, which immediately raises the question, if people from Poland are called Poles, then why aren't those from Holland called Holes?

Unfamiliar with the exalted level of hometown pride, he went around asking anyone who would listen, "So why did people first settle here and decide to stay?" This is somewhat understandable if you appreciate that my husband didn't grow up pulling on wool hats, covering the windows with heavy-gauge plastic, and scraping his car windshield, thus rendering him out of his element in the Great White North. And his visit *was* during a particularly bad winter. However, tribal loyalties prevailed and constituents immediately translated his question into: Why does anyone in his or her right mind live in Buffalo? Leave it to say this was an unpopular conversation starter, or rather, it made him about as welcome as a Saturday turd at Sunday's market, as we like to say in Western New York.

Along similar lines, on minus-ten-degree days Buffalonians do not go around saying, "Is it cold enough for you?" This is considered to be just plain stupid, like saying "eh" to Canadians. On May 13, 2010, when President Obama made his first official visit to Buffalo and said he was happy it wasn't snowing, the otherwise enthusiastic crowd stopped smiling and murmured. It was, after all, following a winter in which the East Coast (including Washington, DC) had been pounded by worse snowstorms than Western New York. Famous CNN reporter Wolf Blitzer, who grew up in Buffalo, explained via Twitter that such remarks are a "NO-NO in Buffalo where folks are sensitive about snow jokes." Much like that proverbial large Italian family, Buffalonians prefer to crack wise about themselves rather than have outsiders do it. But if you insist, at least try to be funny. Or get better speechwriters. Fortunately, Obama had stopped at Duff's Cheektowaga location for a medium order of chicken wings with five extra crispy. A local woman told the commander in chief, "You're a hottie with a smokin' little body," which ended up being the quote heard round the world, and references to all things cold were quickly forgotten.

Western New Yorkers take advantage of winter by skiing, snowboarding, skating, snowmobiling, tobogganing, and sledding—crossover activities occasionally necessary to get the mail or walk the dog. This past winter the first annual Powder Keg Festival offered tubing, snowshoeing, broomball, a snowman-building contest, live music, a soup and chili cook-off, a Saint Bernard–led parade, and the world's largest ice maze. The Guinness World Records judge on hand to measure the ice maze, Amanda Mochan, also judged locals as being "really friendly."

And it's safe to say that cold weather capitals such as Western New York can take credit for the surge in scrapbooking. In pursuit of this perfect indoor hobby, one spends hundreds of dollars on albums, craft punches, stencils, inking tools, eyelet setters, heat-embossing tools, personal die-cut machines and templates, vellum quotes, stamps, rub-ons, edging scissors, pens, lace, wire, glitter, fabric, and ribbon (or a desktop publishing and page layout program with advanced printing options and scanner, if you want to go the digital route), only to realize that a January getaway to the Caribbean would've been less expensive.

Despite a growing season that falls squarely into the stingy category, locals work hard to create award-winning gardens, oftentimes starting those seedlings on the kitchen countertop in Dixie riddle cups in February. Meantime, Buffalo has the largest garden walk in the country. And it's free. Take that, *Forbes* magazine Misery Measure! In fact, the garden walk has been so successful that it was recently transformed into a five-week festival. "Maybe it's just an intense strain of the contagious gardening virus that makes one tiny flower-filled yard turn into a streetful, and a street turn into a neighborhood of gardeners," says local garden expert and author Sally Cunningham. "But I believe it also has to do with all the uncommonly open, friendly people, who share their backyards, flowers, and art in an unprecedented display of hospitality." Furthermore, the stunning Buffalo and Erie County Botanical Gardens features year-round exhibits, guided tours, classes, and special events.

Fishing is a popular year-round sport. It's not for nothing that Lake Erie is known as The Walleye Capital of the World. They're caught by boat, out on the ice, and by casting from shore. You can also fill a cooler with yellow perch and smallmouth bass. If you're looking for a fight, then set your sights on salmon and silver bullet steelhead. If you're looking for a bigger fight, a four-foot-long American alligator weighing eighty pounds was captured in Scajaquada Creek after a four-day hunt back in 2001. Gator aid came in the form of the local dogcatcher, and it was strictly catch and release, as the reptile was given a one-way ticket to a game farm in Florida.

Songwriter Jack Yellen (1892–1991), who emigrated from Poland when he was five years old and grew up in the Buffalo area, scribed "Happy Days Are Here Again," which became Franklin Delano Roosevelt's campaign theme song in 1932, and that of subsequent Democrats, until it was co-opted by Reagan Republicans in 1980. Yellen was always amused by the fact that he wrote the song in just thirty minutes for a relatively unheard of movie called *Chasing Rainbows*, released shortly after the stock market crash of October 1929 marked the onset of the Great Depression.

Although we proudly claim our share of standouts and eccentrics, the denizens of B-lo don't have a tremendous interest in the peccadilloes of politicians and the rehab stints of celebrities. We're more apple brown betty than crème brûlée. The Buffalo and Erie County Library has a first edition of American writer Henry David Thoreau's *Walden* (a.k.a. *Life in the Woods*) in its fabulous rare-books collection. However, Thoreau is not necessarily a hero in my hometown. Buffalonians know that, despite his belief in the divinity of manual labor, Thoreau was wrong about a lot of things. First, you don't traipse off to live alone in a cabin in the woods because (a) it's boring; and (b) you might freeze to death. And let's rather call Nature Boy's cabin a dorm room, because he walked into town almost every day and regularly went home to raid the cookie jar and have his laundry done. Plus, his mom delivered care packages containing homemade meals, pies, and donuts every Saturday.

Thoreau most famously said, "The mass of men lead lives of quiet desperation." Now one could just as easily say this about Bills fans, but I beg to disagree and believe that those fanatics out in subzero weather with DOLPHINS BLOW painted in bright blue across their bare chests are passionate, engaged with humanity, and leading lives of thunderous hope, not only for that Super Bowl ring, but for their children to have good lives in a world devoid of poverty, disease, and brutality. And they're thankful we're not home to the Detroit Lions.

Second-most–famously, Thoreau said, "If a man does not keep pace with his companions, perhaps it is because he hears a different drummer. Let him step to the music which he hears." Now picture a high school marching band stomping around outside on a crisp fall Buffalo day with the French horn player turning at the twenty-yard line, the timpanist heading off toward the concession stand, and all the while everyone is pounding out flats and sharps exactly as they please.

Thoreau died from bronchitis after going out alone on a late-night expedition in a rainstorm to count the rings of a tree stump. Shortly before he passed away, his aunt asked if he'd made peace with God. Thoreau told her that he didn't know they'd quarreled. This seems a good place to mention that he was a Unitarian and helped to advance the belief that man was a part of nature, not separate from it. However, he was such a devout Unitarian that he had to resign being

Unitarian because he felt being Unitarian precluded him from being a joiner.

No, Buffalonians have it right. Join the club and pay the dues. Find others. Celebrate your joys and mourn your losses together. Stick with the herd. Swim with the school. Stay with the flock. And my mother says to wear a hat.

About the Author

© Denise Winters

Laura Pedersen is a former *New York Times* columnist and the best-selling author of ten books, including the award-winning humorous memoir *Buffalo Gal*. She has appeared on *The Oprah Winfrey Show*, *Late Night with David Letterman*, *Good Morning America*, *The Today Show*, *Primetime Live*, CNN, Fox News, and MSNBC. Pedersen divides her time between Amherst, New York, and Manhattan. More information can be found at www.LauraPedersenBooks.com.